AuthorHouse™
1663 Liberty Drive, Suite 200
Bloomington, IN 47403
www.authorhouse.com
Phone: 1-800-839-8640

First published by AuthorHouse 2/26/2009

ISBN: 978-1-4389-3393-1 (sc)

Printed in the United States of America
Bloomington, Indiana

This book is printed on acid-free paper.

FROM THE INDIAN TRACES TO THE DRIVE-INS

An Edgar County Anthology

HARRY PARRISH

authorHOUSE®

THIS WORK IS DEDICATED TO Nellie Jenkins, who taught English literature, American literature, and English composition at Paris High School in the 1960's and 1970's. God rest her soul. She likely now knows who wrote BEOWULF.

> Oh, sweet lady, eye askew,
> Hair in disarray,
> Small, petite, attire by chance
> Each day I think of you
>
> Poets, bards, essayists too
> Beowulf was your forte,
> Dante, Keats, Frost and Yeats,
> Quoth Ye Chaucer and "Velvet Shoes"
>
> As time passed by, our knowledge grew
> As you led us through each phase
> Through grammar texts and rhetoric tests
> Oh, the vocabularies we went through
>
> Page by page and age through age
> Your tutelage carried on
> And age through age, your tutelage sage,
> Unlocked secret doors of written page
>
> And now I write as you said I should
> Many years ago
> And hope to hear your voice so dear
> Saying,"Scribe, well done; I knew you could."

And to Asa Baber, a contributing editor for many years at PLAYBOY MAGAZINE, an English professor, and writer. Asa gave me the confidence to write and urged me on when the words wouldn't come easily. Asa was a good friend taken too early by Lou Gehrig's disease. Maybe you are reading this Asa, may God rest your soul.

CONTENTS

ACKNOWLEDGMENTS

THIS BOOK IS A COMPILATION of articles I researched and wrote over a five-year period. The stories were published by the Paris Beacon Publishing Company and ran in their newspaper. Over the last several years, folks have asked me to combine the articles in book form, and this is the result.

Many things have changed since the original articles were published. I have not updated the articles, nor will I. They should stay as written.

I interviewed hundreds of people, took many pictures, and borrowed many more pictures. The pictures I borrowed were returned to the owners, usually the same day. Most of the folks I interviewed have passed on now, and I think it would probably be an arduous task to try to gather those photos again. I am becoming a bit long in the tooth and will leave that task to someone with more energy.

There are people who should be recognized. My wife, Beverly, has been my proofreader for every undertaking. She is a saint. My typing skills, grammar, and rhetoric leave something to be desired. Thank the stars she is a very good English teacher.

Chris Sunkel is a computer wizard. When I had a problem with my writing program, which is often, she was there to fix my goof, bail me out.

Two more "techies," my daughter Sydney and son-in-law Matt also helped me wend my way through the computer maze. My thanks and my love.

The fall of 2008, I got sick and was homebound for a few weeks. I received a handwritten letter, a thing of the past, from a dear friend, John Tafflinger. I answered his letter and haven't put down my pen since. You got me writin' again Jar-head, thanks!

To all of you still around who contributed to these efforts, thank you very, very much.

TRACES OF OUR ANCESTORS

WHILE DRIVING THE WINDING BACK roads of east central Illinois and western Indiana, enjoying the splendors of fall, searching for that perfect autumn photo or bouquet of bittersweet, chances are you traveled some of the original trails that our ancestors followed to the area that is now Edgar County, Illinois.

Adin Baber, now deceased, was a historian and author from Kansas, Illinois. In 1965, he wrote, "As early as 1913, after acquiring a used Model T, I "tooled" it over the grass grown relics and unimproved dusty sections of the old Paris Springfield road. There is for me a sentient intangible pleasure in retracing the trails of the pioneers". So too, for me.

Earlier in the 1930s, Mr. Baber had followed the Kaskaskia Detroit Trace and wrote a monograph for the Illinois State Historical Society, Vol. XXV, which was published in 1932. That manuscript and the unpublished 1965 work were invaluable tools in preparing this article. The desire to investigate these earliest trails and the puzzlement of why anyone would uproot his family lock, stock, and barrel to travel to an unexplored region encountering hostiles, bears, panthers, and hordes of insects, let alone the inconvenience of living in a covered wagon, prompted me to seek some answers.

Of course, the reasons men pulled up stakes and subjected their families to the trials and tribulations of pioneer travel are as unique as each individual, and most are well documented: religious persecution, such as the Mormons' exodus from Illinois to Utah; ethnic persecution; riches; the gold rush of '49; and the plagues that drove families from the East to Kentucky and Tennessee.

H. C. Bradsbury describes the "first" white man to set foot into Vigo County, Indiana, as like "a wandering Jew" he pursued his aimless course "caring little for the past and nothing of the future". He eked out his existence hunting the abundant game; buffalo, deer and waterfowl abounded. And his encounters with the Indians, such as the Kickapoo, Sauteurs, Sac and others, were mostly of a friendly nature. It would be much later before the Indian nations took up arms against the encroaching white settlers.

Webster defines a trail as, "a beaten path; also, a marked path through the woods". Indeed, a trail is shaped by the terrain it follows. Through a forest it might be narrow, as dictated by the density of the trees, widening as the trees thin into savannas and prairies. But can you imagine a trail a mile wide? The trails that led through the Grand Prairie were in places that wide because of the wet soil. The prairie grass was dense and tall, creating shade that hindered the evaporation process. A man on horseback could not see over those grasses. Victor Collot wrote in 1796, "We measured some stalks which were twenty-one feet high". The terrain was flat, preventing drainage. Therefore, the wild game and man would, as moisture dictated, bypass the wettest areas. As the grass was beaten down, water surfaced, creating impassable mud holes that had to be skirted for drier footing, thus creating yet a wider trail. The trails those first settlers used were buffalo traces that meandered from watering hole to watering hole, to salt licks, or to high ground to escape the voracious insects. Hulbert, in his writings, names the buffalo as "the greatest pathfinder on the North American continent".

> From *Wilson's History of DuBois County:* "the buffalo was a large, heavy animal with
> a comparatively small foot. He could not cross low, swampy, marshy land, and be-
> ing gregarious, he could not remain long in one place, for hundreds and sometimes
> thousands of them ranged together. Their pastures vanished rapidly, and they had
> to move frequently. Buffalo roads, therefore, were very definitely marked and well
> beaten. The Miami Indian name for a buffalo road was 'Lan an zo ki mi wi'".

The small feet of these animals, along with their heavy bodies, necessitated their roads following the highlands, the ridges, or watersheds. The Indians followed these trails because they were open and occasionally furnished game. When the white man came as an explorer, hunter or settler, he also followed these lines of least resistance. The buffalo avoided the hill and the swamp, and therefore took to the ridge or to the valley. He was a good civil engineer and pathfinder. In fact, he found the road and man followed in his footsteps.

In the mid-1600s, Claude Allouez, M. Claude Dablon and James Marquette founded the mission at Sault Ste. Marie. Marquette and Joliet would later cross Lake Illinois, now Lake Michigan, to Green Bay, Wisconsin, in search of "the great river", the Mississippi. Outposts were established. In 1680, Fort Crevecoeur was built by LaSalle at Pim i te wi, now Lake Peoria on the Illinois River. Later forts were established at Kaskaskia, on the Mississippi, and at Vincennes and Quiatanon on the Oubache. It was only natural that those forts be connected by a network of trails. Parts of these trails had been in existence for hundreds of years, used first by game, then by man. Two of those early buffalo trails used by early man and later by the settlers on their way to the Northwest Territory intersect in northwest Edgar County at Palermo, which was then known as Hickory Grove. These trails were Lake Peoria (Ft. Clark) and Wabash Trail and the Detroit-Kaskaskia Trace. The third major trace that tracked through eastern Edgar County was Hubbard's Trace, which was an extension of the Old Buffalo Trace, which was also known as "Vincennes

Trace", "Trace To The Falls", the Louisville Trace, or the Old Indian Trace. By whatever name it was referred to, its existence was evident as early as 1718, when M. de Vaudreuil, then governor of Canada, traveled over it. He wrote about the great number of bison encountered on their route. At times it was necessary to discharge their weapons to disperse the large herds of animals so they could proceed along their way.

There is an excellent account of traveling over this rigorous trail that breached the one hundred and ten miles from Louisville, Kentucky, to Vincennes, Indiana, in 1804. Edward Hempstead, an attorney who settled in Vincennes that year, penned to Jared Mansfield, the newly appointed Surveyor General in charge of laying out the Vincennes Tract:

> "The journey from Louisville, here would be somewhat disagreeable to a female . . . , Perhaps you Sir might not think so, but I am positive, that Mrs. Mansfield could not easily reconcile herself to the inconvenience of it-You are obliged to furnish yourself at Louisville with provisions for yourself and forage for your horses, as there is no place at which they can be obtained on the road.

> "The journey is commonly performed in three days, at night you are obliged to lodge on the ground and the whole way is nothing but a wilderness, with no road but a good footpath".

If Jared Mansfield was optimistic about how his wife would fare on the trail, at least one woman enjoyed traveling under the rigors the trace offered. Lieutenant Josiah Bacon's wife, Lydia, kept a journal of their travels from Vincennes to Louisville in 1812.

> On May 14, that year she wrote:" I like traveling on horseback and slept finely last night, for the first time in my life, with a bear skin for our bedstead & a buffalo robe for our bed.

> May 19:" 19th bright sun, all going on in good health & spirits, but my feelings are somewhat tried seeing the poor soldier's wives trudging on foot, some of the way mud up to their knees, & a little child in their arms, only 4 or 5 wagons allowed to carry the baggage, the poor women of course have to suffer, I should think it would kill them . . . "

> Her journal continues:" I suppose you will be anxious to know what we have to eat, how we carry conveniences to eat out of & and how we cook- we live very well as to the quality of our victuals & have enough, plenty of elegant bacon (nothing better) in this part of the world. We have a pack horse who carries a pair of mess

boxes made with separate apartments to hold cups plates & ccc & our tea and sugar in cannisters, & our table is the hind board of a waggon set on a portable cricket made like a cot bedstead, our candle is a bayonet reversed with the point in the ground, the part which goes on the gun serves admirably for a socket to put the candle in."

By the turn of the nineteenth century, the great trailblazer, the American bison, had all but vanished from Illinois. Two factors were responsible for his disappearance: hunting pressure and two abnormally severe winters.Before the white man arrived, the Indians had difficulty killing the buffalo with only bows and arrows. In December of 1679, LaSalle and his party were exploring the Illinois River Valley and were in need of meat. They knew the buffalo were plentiful but could find none because the Miamis had fired the prairie for their autumn hunt. Hennepin wrote:

"When they (the Miamis) see a herd, they gather in great numbers and set fire to the grass everywhere around these animals, except some passages which they leave on purpose, and where they take post with their bows and arrows. The buffalo, seeking to escape the fire, are thus compelled to pass near these Indians, who sometimes kill as many as a hundred and twenty in a day . . ."

But when the white explorers and settlers arrived, the kill increased greatly because of the rifle. Moyers wrote in 1931 that, "from early 1703, until April 1704, a party of French hunters worked the Big Muddy and Wabash Rivers, as well as the Tennessee, Cumberland, and Caster Rivers, and Apple Creek and took the skins from thirteen-thousand bison".

In this area buffalo were still in existence in 1765. George Groghan made the following entry in his journal of June 18, 1765, of his trek from Vincennes to Quiatanon on the Wabash:

"We traveled through a prodigious large meadow, called the Pyankeshaw's hunting ground. Here is no wood to be seen, and the country appears like an ocean. The ground is exceedingly rich and partially overgrown with wild hemp. The land is well watered and full of buffalo, deer, bears, and all kinds of wild game."

If the increase in hunting pressure wasn't enough, severe winter weather pushed the bison from the Illinois prairie. Indian legend refers to a great snow that all but eliminated the buffalo before the turn of the century. The legend is substantiated by an account given by Hicks writing on the history of Kendall County, 1763. "The snow fell, it is said, twelve feet deep-the severest winter ever known- and the buffaloes, cut off from their supplies, wholly perished". In the winter of 1806–1807, thousands of buffalo in the Mississippi Valley perished. Marsh, in reviewing the family history of Mercer County says, "The buffalo could swim the Mississippi River but herds sometimes broke through the ice in the winter". The family journal records that 7,380 buffalo carcasses were counted on the river's shore on May 2, 1807, having fallen through the ice the winter past. And then came the harshest winter ever recorded.

Prior to 1830, the settlers had winter pastured their livestock in the open with little or no shelter provided for them. Wheat and corn were stacked in the fields to be husked as needed. Wood was stacked and left in the woods to be carried home as needed. Then in the winter of 1830, on the twentieth of December cold rain began to fall. The day before Christmas the rain turned to snow. This description of that winter is from excerpts of "The Winter of the Deep Snow", by Eleanor Atkinson.

"The wildest imagination could not have dreamed that this first fall of snow was merely the overture to a winter of continuous storm. The first white mantle still lay unsullied on the frozen prairie, in a profound hush of nature, when the meteorological opera opened with a crash on the thirtieth of December.

"A furious gale, bitter cold, a blinding, swirling blur of snow, and leaden, lowering skies, combined to make this storm a thing to paralyze that prairie country. It seems to have continued for days, unabated-a wonder at first, then a terror, a benumbing horror as it became a menace to life of men and animals. The food was in the fields, the fuel in the woods, the cattle huddled and perishing of cold and starvation, in the open. It snowed almost daily, up to the middle of February. No morning dawned for many a day when the thermometer registered less than twelve degrees below zero. It took a man an entire day to dig enough corn out of frozen shocks to keep a few cattle alive for a few days. Famishing deer and small game were easily obtained, but crops were lost, much of the livestock perished, and many kinds of small game were very nearly exterminated."

And so by 1830, the "Great Trailblazer" had all but vanished from this area, but his legacy remained, the interstates of the times connected by the lesser routes made by smaller game and by man.

Four major trails cut through Edgar County by the time our first ancestors arrived here. Blazed by bison and smaller game, those trails had been in existence for hundreds of years and were well known and used in the earliest years by Indians, trappers and missionaries. The first settlers who arrived in Edgar County would have likely known by word of mouth what sort of trails existed. They would have known the conditions of the trails, when they could best travel over them, and generally in which direction they led. Vincennes could have been called the gateway to the Great

Northwest. Settlers from the East traveled Boone's Trace through the Cumberland Gap to the Falls of the Ohio, thence over the Buffalo Trace to Vincennes.

Two trails of importance led north from Vincennes, one on each bank of the Wabash. The east bank trail led north to Fort Harrison (Terre Haute), then on to Fort Quiatenon, where it intersected with the Kaskaskia-Fort Detroit Trace. Fort Quiatenon was established in 1717, five miles southwest of modern Lafayette, Indiana, on the Wabash River.

In 1763, Chief Pontiac set out to drive the Europeans back behind the Appalachian Mountains. Pontiac's confederation of tribes attacked twelve frontier outposts and successfully captured eight of them, including Quiatenon which fell without a shot being fired. The Indians simply walked in and took the poorly manned fort. "Pontiac's Uprising" came to an end as a result of Pontiac and Croghan's powwow at Hickory Grove in Edgar County. The treaty negotiated there was later signed at Quiatenon. After that signing, and all was at rest, Quiatenon was not regarrisoned. In 1778, just twelve families of whites remained at Quiatenon neighbored by over a thousand Wea Indians that were camped across the Oubache.

The trail on the west bank of the river was an extension of the Vincennes Trace and was also known as Hubbard's Trace. In the autumn of 1823, Gurdon S. Hubbard was named superintendent of the American Fur Company. His base of operation was located on the Iroquois River at Old Bunkum, now known as Iroquois, Illinois.

The following is from an article written in 1923 by Milo M. Quafe, titled "Chicago's Highways Old And New":

> "Leaving Chicago with a pack-train of fifty ponies, which had been purchased from Chief Big Foot's village at the head of Lake Geneva, he marked out the trail to his Iroquois River post.

> "From his station at Old Bunkum Hubbard continued for several years to carry on his trading activities. A farm of eighty acres was put under cultivation, the first in Iroquois County, a log house, together with the necessary outbuildings was erected, and the establishment became the headquarters for the trade of a wide region. Hubbard opened a line of trading stations southward along the Indian trail almost to the mouth of the Wabash River, the post at Danville being the most important inland station.

> "As settlements increased along the line of trading posts the Indian trade fell off, and Hubbard gradually gave up the southern posts.

"Hubbard built the first frame building—a storehouse—ever erected in Danville, Illinois. For over fifty years, it continued to stand on the south side of the public square and became the headquarters for the Indian trade for the surrounding region. The red men would file into town on their ponies, sometimes fifty or a hundred in number, with their furs, their squaws, and papooses, and for several days, business would be brisk at Hubbard's corner of the square. The days of the Indian were numbered, however, and in 1832, Hubbard converted his stock into 'white goods' as merchandise for white people was called. The following year he removed to Chicago where for over a half a century he continued a leading citizen of the place."

The fur trader's life was one of hardship and danger from both the red man and from nature. Consider this, from Samuel McCoy: "The cougar! The traveler threading his lonely way through the wilderness heard its wild screaming, like the horrid wailing of a damned soul, far off in the forest aisles, and shuddered; or he might even catch sight of the fearful animal, a tawny yellow shape, larger than the largest dog, its tremendous muscles rippling beneath its smooth coat, its body sunk low to the ground, its huge steel-clawed feet falling lightly as thistle-down upon the forest turf; gliding among the tree trunks with a fearful beautiful grace, bounding with leaps of twenty, thirty feet along the ground, or running lightly along the branches of the trees, there to crouch for long hours, unseen, silent; the motionless cruel heart of the cruel wilderness, waiting for its prey; at last to leap down upon a deer, the woodsman or the pioneer who passed beneath, and falling like a thunderbolt, to tear open with claw and fang, throat and artery, and to plunge its dripping muzzle into warm blood. Tecumseh, 'the cougar about to spring.'"

From Milo Quaife: " While in Indian country he (Hubbard) habitually wore a buckskin hunting shirt or a blue capote belted at the waste with a sash, or buckskin belt, in which was carried a knife and a sheath, a tomahawk, and a tobacco-pouch made of mink or otter skin. In this pouch was a flint and steel, together with a piece of punk, to be used in striking a fire. Underneath the outer garment was a calico shirt, breech-cloth, and buckskin leggings. On his feet were moccasins and pieces of blanket wrapped around to take the place of stockings. His head was bare, and his hair long and matted. In winter he carried a blanket, which he sometimes wore in Indian fashion. Clad in such garb, with face and hands browned by toil and exposure to the elements, there was but little outward appearance to distinguish the trader from the savage."

There are numerous stories about the adventures of Gurdon Hubbard, but one that stands out from his fur-trading days along the trace is the story of Watseka. This again from "Chicago's Highways Old And New".

"Watseka was born at the Indian village on the site of Old Bunkum about the year 1810. Competition was fierce in the Indian trade, and the trader who could win the friendship of a chief enjoyed an advantage over his competitors which was not to be ignored. In savage, as in civilized life, the favor of royalty is best secured and cemented through marriage alliances. In accordance with the custom of the forest, Hubbard entered upon a marriage of convenience by taking to wife a relative of Tamin, chief of the Kankakee band of Potawatomi. It was Tamin's first desire that Hubbard should wed his own daughter, but for reasons which may easily be imagined the latter declined this alliance. Instead he indicated his willingness to marry Tamin's niece, Watseka, then a child of ten years of age. A pledge to do so was given, and when the girl had arrived at the age of fourteen or fifteen years she was brought to Hubbard by her mother and the marriage was consummated.

" Over this union, as over the career of Watseka, hovers much of pathos and trage-dy. Watseka was a beautiful and intelligent girl, and Hubbard in after years testified to the ideal character of his union with her. It lasted about two years, during which a daughter was born and died. The advancing tide of white settlement spelled the doom of the Indian trade, and Hubbard, who possessed abundant foresight and shrewdness, laid his plans for abandoning his calling. This would involve severing his connection with Watseka's tribe and taking up life anew in a civilized com-munity. Under these circumstances the couple separated by mutual agreement, 'in perfect friendship", according to Hubbard. His account of the transaction is en-titled to entire credit, yet one can readily imagine that it was dictated more by the strong-willed husband, member of the dominate race and sex, than by a submis-sive wife. Viewed from any angle it was a hard situation, and Watseka doubtless had the sense to perceive than acquiescence in her husband's wishes was the only course open to her. After the separation from Hubbard she became the wife of Noel Levasseur, whom Hubbard left in charge of his post at bunkum. After living with Levasseur for almost a decade and bearing him several children, this union was also dissolved, apparently much as the one with Hubbard had been. Watseka, still a comparatively young woman, now joined the remnant of the tribe in Kansas, while Levasseur, like Hubbard, remained in Illinois and contracted a new marriage alliance, this time with a white woman."

The following is a tale related by Mr. James W. Kern, an attorney of Watseka, Illinois, as was retold in Adin Baber's From Prairie Grass to Cornfields:

"Just after the Civil War ended, Mr. Kern's mother was giving a tea party to three of her companions and as they sat in the yard there came through the front gate, as they thought, an old Gypsy woman, But as the woman approached they recognized Watseka. She had walked all the way from Kansas to visit the graves of her children.

"The Kerns kept her over night; the next morning Mrs. Kern filled a large basket with food, enough for several days. Mr. Kern hitched his horses to his road wagon and took Watseka up river about ten miles to the site of the old trading post. Here, nearby, Watseka pointed out the location of her children's graves under a large Oak tree. She desired to be left there with them so Mr. Kern returned home. Watseka remained at the tree for three days then walked back to town, to the Kerns.

"She remained in the town all summer and worked for Mrs. Kern's friends and for other women, helping out at their house cleaning and home chores of washing clothes and dishes for her keep.

"When winter drew nigh, some of the men of the town considered that better than to keep her or send her to the county poor farm, she should be sent back to her own tribe in the State of Kansas. Mr. Kern's father and others took up a collection, tickets on the trains were purchased, food to last the few day's trip was furnished, and she was put on the cars to be carried to Kansas, where she later died; her grave, like those of her children is now unknown."

In 1834, the Illinois legislature authorized a road to be built between Vincennes and Chicago. The commissioners who located the road wanted a straighter line between the two cities and better ground than Hubbard's Trace, but were forced to follow the old track with little deviation. In 1834, the few farmers who inhabited this area had long distances to travel to sell their commodities. Chicago was becoming a major trade center by then and at least two families from this area traveled Hubbard's Trace to sell their products there.

William Forsythe had settled in northern Clark County near the trace. The Kimble family settled just north of Paris. Both families had apple orchards. In early autumn, the families would pack the apples into barrels, load them onto large wagons hitched to four horses, and start the five-day journey to Chicago. The trip was not to be taken lightly. There were four river crossings between Edgar County and Chicago to negotiate, and the many lesser creeks could at times be formidable obstacles themselves.On these journeys it was not uncommon for horses or oxen to injure themselves while crossing the rivers or fighting through the muck. Axles on the wagons would often break, and packing a spare wheel was a must. After arriving in Chicago and disposing of their load at hopefully a good price, the wagoneers would start back home with the staples that had been ordered from their surrounding neighbors. One staple that was always in demand was salt. On the return trip the wagons would stop at the salt works on the Little Vermillion River. Salt was bought by the barrel, loaded onto the wagons, then carried home and dispensed to those that had ordered it.

This is an account of a trip to Chicago taken in 1832, as related by David S. Curtis, the son of Joseph and Hannah Curtis. Joseph was a nurseryman who had located on the north fork of Coal Creek in modern Hunter Township. The story is taken from a history written by Lloyd Lewis several years ago entitled North Arm Neighborhood, "The Way It Used To Be":

> "My first trip to Chicago was in 1834. We had two six ox teams loaded with sixty bushels of sweet potatoes each. The wagons were of the old Pennsylvania linchpin style with very large and heavy beds. Our expenses on such a trip were very light, our oxen being unyoked at night to graze at leisure. We kept a horse along which to hunt up the oxen in the morning. They would occasionally give us trouble in finding them. We had to encounter swamps almost innumerable, doubling our teams to extricate ourselves from uncomfortable situations, making but few miles advance some days. We went by what was called the Hickory Creek route. For about twelve miles before reaching Chicago everything was covered with water except one narrow ridge where we availed ourselves of the opportunity to gather up some roots that were on the ridge, made a fire, boiled our coffee, ate our lunch, rested our teams, and again waded into the water. In the evening we encamped at Wright's Grove on the Chicago River about two miles from the little village of Chicago, at that time containing about four or five hundred inhabitants."

The story goes on to say that they had no problem selling the potatoes. They were delayed in Chicago on their return trip. They had wanted to load salt, three-fifty a barrel, but the boat was late arriving. When the entourage finally departed for home, more problems were encountered. This again from Lloyd Lewis' telling:

> "At Blue Island we found a man with a four horse team who had been waiting several days for someone to come along and pull him out of the miserable swamp. Horses were not at all suited for those swamps, but for crossing swollen streams were very much better than oxen, since the oxen would become almost unmanage-

able in the water. So, with the understanding that he would pilot us out of the stream, we helped him out of his unpleasant dilemma."

David Shelby Curtis was born July 1, 1819, and died January 28, 1899, of "organic heart decease." The year that he wrote this account is unknown but his epilogue is poignant:

"Thus was one of the most eventful trips of my life. To look back on my first trip to Chicago, then a mere village and to see it the second city of the nation as to population and first in commercial importance, to look at the dense population in these broad prairies once thought uninhabitable, to take into account what I have seen in the progress of my native state, I am older than Methuselah, for in his life of 969 years he never saw so much".

Terre Haute, Indiana, also played an important role in the early migration westward. Settlers could arrive at Terre Haute from the south on the Wabash River or via the Vincennes-Quiatanon Trace. Some would come from the northeastern part of the country via the Detroit-Kaskaskia Trace, thence south on the Quiatanon Trace.

Three major trails led into Edgar County from the Terre Haute area. These were the Fort Clark-Wabash Trace, the oldest; the Terre Haute-North Arm Wagon Road, and the Durkees Ferry Trace.

The first ferry across the Wabash River was located just north of Terre Haute at modern Tecumseh. It was established August 11, 1818, by Dr. John Durkee and Salmon Lusk on land owned by Durkee in Fayette Township. The Vigo County Court commission of the ferry reads in part:

"It is hereby established that the proprietors thereof procure and keep for the succeeding year one good flat boat sufficient for the transportation of a loaded waggon and four horses, also one skiff or pirogue together with a sufficient number of hands for manning the same".

The crossing fees were seasonal: from May until December for a man and a horse, twenty-five cents; from December until May the fee was thirty-seven and a half cents for a wagon and a horse and twelve and a half cents for each additional horse. Hogs and sheep were three and a half cents each. In 1824, Dr. Durkee relocated to Tippecanoe County. He was a prominent landowner and farmer. His son, David F. Durkee, was the first sheriff of Tippecanoe County. Dr. Durkee died February 26, 1834, at the age of sixty-four.But his legacy, Durkee's Ferry Trace, lives on today. Although the ferry is no longer in existence, one can still find evidence of it today and travel most of the original trace that leads from the river to Paris. The trace leads from Tecumseh,

Indiana, northwest through Fayette Township and crosses the Indiana-Illinois state line at modern Libertyville. Route 150 actually follows part of the trace until it deviates at New Goshen. Crossing the state line, the trace enters Stratton Township at section 33 and follows the northern tree line for some two miles, where it then crosses a mile of prairie to reenter the woods at modern Blackburn Cemetery. From the cemetery, the trail meanders westward until it reaches Paris, probably what is now the Blackhawk Park area, which in prior years had been a major camp and meeting area for the Kickapoo Indian Tribes.

It is not known to me if Indians had names for individual trails, maybe. Modern man does, and because of this, the part of the trail called Durkee's Ferry ended at Paris. But it did not. The trail, however, continued to meander southwestward along the tree line, skirting the prairie to modern Grandview, thence westward through the "Gap," another meeting place of the Kickapoos in Kansas Township. It was here at the Gap that the last of the Kickapoo tribe camped for the last time in Edgar County. The year was 1831, and the tribe was being relocated to the state of Kansas. There were several hundred Indians gathered at the Gap to listen to a final sermon given by Father Buel. Here is an account of that meeting and the meal that followed, given by William Darnall, who was attending the meeting.

"This was the last meeting held by these people before their removal from these parts. The meeting was a most interesting and exciting one. Father Buel was on hand and preached from his chart one of his peculiarly entertaining discourses, while one of his assistants, who spoke both languages, translated for the benefit of those who had not learned to speak English. The excitement and confusion which attended the graphic description of the two opposite states of man, beyond the dark river, can better be conceived than described. Suffice it to say, that no Methodist revival which I ever attended or heard described, compared with that manifested by those poor, ignorant creatures. After services a great dinner was partaken of. This had been cooking in large camp-kettles all the fore-noon. It consisted of meats of various kinds, boiled with wheat and herbs of different sorts, until the whole mass was cooked to the consistency of thick soup, or more nearly of mush. Some of the white boys, by invitation, had intended to eat with them; but when they saw the meat, on which the flies had not only deposited their eggs, but the eggs had actually hatched, and the skippers traveled gaily up and down, flung into the kettle, meat, eggs and all, we concluded we were not so hungry as we thought we had been and respectfully declined. The savory mess was swallowed by the reds with evident relish, some eating from dishes, and more dipping with wooden spoons or dirty hands from the kettles." Not long after that meeting the entire band along with others from Indiana were removed to Kansas State.

It was a custom of Indians, when they broke camp, to bend over and turn up a sapling tree. This was likely a sign to those following of their being there before, or more likely marking hallowed ground. The last time the Kickapoo left the Gap, there were no saplings sprung. Today Illinois Route Sixteen follows that trail for a few miles just west of Paris.

The trail which Durkee's Ferry Trace followed is ancient. The other two trails leading into Illinois from the Terre Haute area, the Terre Haute-North Arm Wagon Road and the Wabash River-Lake Peoria Trail, follow the same line in places.The three run almost parallel through Vigo County, Indiana, from the river westward to the Illinois line. The trail enters Illinois at just north of Sandford in Section 21, Twp 13N, Rg. 11W. There was until recently a barn in that section, built on the bias and on or very near that trace. The wagon road proceeds northwesterly through land owned in the past by the Trogdon family at Section.1, Twp. 13N, Rg. 11W. There the two traces merge with the Durkee's Ferry Trace and then meander westward to the Blackhawk Park area. The Blackhawk Park area evidently played a major role in the lives of ancient civilizations. All four major trails that led into this area converge at the park. The game was plentiful, as shown by the many buffalo wallows found in northern Paris Township. Artifacts dating to before 1000 B.C. have been found in the immediate area, and the spring at Blackhawk Park is still flowing as I write this.

The Wabash River-Fort Clark Trace was an original buffalo trace. Buffalo migrated from the forests of southeastern Edgar County to the northwest to avail themselves of the rich prairie grasses. This from Adin Baber's From Prairie Grass To Cornfield;

> "It is altogether fitting that Illinois be called the Prairie State. It was home to the buffalo, with its tall grasses, the Big Bluestem and its shorter cousins, the Andro-pogans which waved with the wind as the grazing animals filled their paunches with the lush grass. This grass dried into hay for the wintertime provender and the buffalo, woolly-coated against the blizzards, pawed the snow aside to eat their fill. When warm weather came, they shed their shaggy, heavy winter coats by rubbing their itching sides against the big cottonwood trees along the streams. Such "rub-bing place" trees were often debarked around the trunks.

> "With the loss of their coats they were attacked by the voracious insects, the buf-falo gnats. Audubon, in one of his Episodes, tells of the death of his horse from the stings of the buffalo gnats, when he crossed the prairies of southern Illinois. The

buffalo wallowed in the miry mud of the sloughs by lying on their backs, kicking with a hind leg, and spinning to plaster their molted hides against the gnats.

"The constant carrying away of mud from the buffalo wallows left the depressions now called ponds, although many have long since been tapped with tile to be drained."

From Blackhawk Park, the Fort Clark-Wabash River Trace angled northwest meandering between the swamps and buffalo wallows until it reached Mulberry Grove, modern Garland. From there the trace took a more northerly track to Patch Grove, now Hume, and thence on to Hickory Grove, where it intersected the Detroit-Kaskaskia Trace. The trace exited Edgar County at the northwest quarter of Sec.1, Twp.16N, Rg14W, into Vermilion County.

Before the white man inhabited the Hickory Grove area, the grove was an important meeting place of various Indian tribes. The Kickapoo had a camp there. There were four large springs that provided ample water, and small game abounded. There in 1765, a British colonel, George Croghan, a deputy superintendent of Indian affairs for the British government, made a preliminary treaty with Pontiac, chief of the Ottawas and leader of a large confederation of Indians. One of the French translators at that meeting was Francis G. Greene. For his reward for helping secure that treaty, which was later signed at Fort Quiatanon, he was awarded a section of land located in now Young America Township. The land lies just north and east of Palermo and, in part, is still owned by Philip Greene, a direct descendant of Francis. The acreage is the highest point in the state of Illinois. One of the original obelisks placed by the land surveyors in 1825 still stands on that farm. Curiously, the obelisk is protected by a machine shed that was inadvertently built over it several years ago. The obelisk was just recently discovered.

The first pioneers to enter the Edgar County area from the hardwood forests of the East and Southeast ventured into an ocean of grass that stretched miles into the heartland of the Illinois country.

In 1822, Daniel Reed had made his way into this prairie from Montgomery County, Kentucky. He ventured northwest from the Wabash River following the Wabash-Fort Clark Trace. His trek would lead him through the prairie skirting Mulberry Grove and its large lake. Mulberry Grove is known as Garland today. From that grove, he proceeded north to Patch Grove, now Hume, and thence north to Hickory Grove, where he settled and built a cabin.

This is from a speech given at the dedication ceremony of the Palermo Historical Marker by Mrs. D. A. Richardson, October 17, 1924. Her husband came to the area from Monroe County, Indiana, when he was nine years old in a "Prairie Schooner."

"Wild turkey, prairie chickens, quail, ducks, geese, squirrel, rabbit, and deer were plentiful and were so tame that many times they could be shot from the cabin door. If eggs were wanted it was an easy matter to go out around the ponds which were numerous and come in with a hat or basket full of eggs of the wild duck, goose or pheasant. There was an abundance of nuts and wild fruits, berries, crabapple, grapes, plums, persimmons, and paw-paws."

Daniel Reed did not go hungry, nor was he lonesome. Although he was the lone white man in the area at that time, he was neighbored by three hundred Indians who camped nearby. In 1822, Hickory Grove consisted of fifteen hundred acres of hardwoods. By 1837, the migration of settlers had rapidly increased, and the prairie forest had been reduced to less than one hundred acres.

The Detroit-Kaskaskia Trail cut through Edgar County at Hickory Grove. It enters from Vermilion County two miles northeast of Palermo in Section Five of Young America Township, proceeds southwest through Palermo and exits into Douglas County. From a paper written by Dr. J. B. Ruyle on the trace:

"History holds no more romantic tale than the story of the men and women whose feet wore down the hard sod and underlined the Kaskaskia Trail. The black-robed Jesuit, counting his beads as he treads the weary miles, sober-clad nuns of the Ursulines, the settler and outlaw, fair patrician women and outpouring riffraff from the Saltpetrier and other hospitals of Paris; renegade Girty, great patriots like George Rogers Clark, Major Croghan, William Henry Harrison. Here passed Pontiac, Gomo, Little Bird, Tecumseh, and his brother, the one-eyed prophet. Along the trail captive women and children have been hurried into distant villages, and a life of slavery. On this trail have stumbled white settlers and soldiers, driven like cattle, to furnish sport for the Indian squaws, before dying at the stake. It has seen grave warriors stalking ahead of bundle-laden squaws, behind them hardy ponies dragging the teepee, digging up the soft earth. It resounded to the creak of the Conestoga wagon, slowly winding its way across the prairie. Along its course have been seen the uniforms of the French grenadiers, British Highlanders, the buff and blue of the Continental troops. Here traded Clark's backwoodsmen, the "Long Knives" in moccasins and fringed hunting shirts. Here have marched troops under the yellow flag of Spain, the fleur de lis of LaBelle France, the cross of Saint George, and the American Stars and Stripes".

There is a large stone marker commemorating the trail set on the Vermilion-Edgar County line two miles northeast of Palermo, on land once owned by Mr. and Mrs. Dan Mahoney. Until recently, one could still see the ruts from the wagons that had passed through their front yard. In the late 1800s, Mr. Mahoney planted a row of maple trees on each side of the trail in his yard, but today, only one tree remains.

Another of the ancient trails was a footpath and game trail that led southwest from Clinton, Indiana. In Edgar County, the trail joined the Fort Clark-Wabash River Trace just east of Paris at Sugar Creek. This is the trail that the Mormon leader Joseph Smith led a large band of his followers over in May of 1834. The group was on their way to Missouri, and the following passages are from Joseph Smith's diary. "Saturday, May 24.—We crossed the Wabash River at Clinton in ferry boats, in quick time, and pushed on to the state line, where we arrived late in the evening, and encamped in an oak opening in Edgar County Illinois.

"Sunday, May 25.- We had no meeting, but attended to washing, baking, and preparing to resume our journey. A man in disguise, having on an old seal skin cap, came into our camp. He swore we were going up to Jackson County, and that we would never get over the Mississippi River alive. It was evident he was a spy, and I recollect having seen him in Jackson County, Missouri.

"Monday, May 26.- A very hot day. We traveled through Paris and across a sixteen mile prairie; at noon we stopped to bait at a slough, about six miles from the timber, having no water to drink but such as was filled with living animals commonly called wigglers, and as we did not like to swallow them we strained the water before using it. This was the first prairie of any extent that we had come to on our journey, and was a great curiosity to many of the brethren. It was so very level that the deer miles off appeared but a short distance away; some of the brethren started out in pursuit before they were apprised of their mistake as to the distance. We continued our march, pulling our wagons through a small creek with ropes, and came to the house of Mr. Wayne, the only settler in the vicinity, where we found a well of water, which was one of the greatest comforts we could have received, as we were almost famished, and it was a long time before we could, or dared to satisfy our thirst."

Of course the end result of that Mormon trek is well documented. This writer tried to trace the lineage of the Mr. Wayne alluded to in the diary, but that effort ended in a blind alley. Possibly, the entourage had by that time entered Coles County.

As early as 1823, a petition was submitted to the Edgar County court by Thomas Cary of Grandview, for a road from Paris in a southwest direction to the county line and then to connect with the road to the state capital, then in Vandalia, Illinois.

> Adin Baber: "This road was in away only the recognition and widening of the earlier Kickapoo Indian trail that followed the timber lines on the south and skirted the miles and miles of the Grand Prairie that lay to the north. The Indian trail ran from the big spring in present Twin Lakes Park, where the Kickapoo Indians camped, southwest past the Gap in present Kansas Township, where other Kickapoos lived and, crossing the Ambraw River at later Parker's Ford, went to the Kaskaskia River and beyond to the chain of rocks on the Mississippi."

Aric Sutherland was the first settler in now what is Grandview Township. A description of what he must have seen as he trekked southwest on the old trace is given in Forbes History of Edgar County 1879:

> "From a distance, the light seems to break in upon the hitherto dusky wood, and in a few minutes we are on the edge of the prairie, and we all exclaim, with one accord, What a grand view! Certainly no finer scene could well be imagined than that which stretches out to the west, north, and south. It is true, there are none of those rugged scenes of grandeur which distinguish the country further east, and over which artists and poets are wont to ponder in admiration; but rather the quiet beauty of rounded outlines, clothed with the grassy plain, and clumps of trees, arranged in almost park-like order."

And that leads us to the last of the major ancient traces that criss-crossed through the heart of Edgar County.

This trace entered the county from Indiana at Section Sixteen, in the southeast corner of Elbridge Township. The trail, now known as the Lower Terre Haute Road, traveled northwest, crossed Sugar Creek, and then climbed the hill that led to the top of the terminal moraine, which was formed by the Wisconsinan Glacial Period from fifteen to fifty thousand years ago. That ridge extends from just east of the town of Elbridge and westerly to a point south of Paris on the Preston Road, which in ancient times followed Big Creek.

Like Adin Baber, who in 1913 "tooled" across these ancient traces in his Model T, this writer traveled this particular trail on a rainy February day eighty-eight years later. It is the only remaining trail that one can follow in its entirety today. The trail has not changed in centuries and has only minor deviations by modern man. In fact, following the trace across the county, you will find only two miles of straight road, and those two miles are up- and downhill. This foot trail splits just south of modern Nevins; the right hand branch of the foot and game trail leads into the Blackhawk Park area. The trail that leads west proceeds to the bottoms of Big Creek, where it intersects with what was later known as Hubbard's Trace. From the ford at Pitchers Hill, the trail leads on to the town of Grandview, where it joins the trail leading westward from Blackhawk Park. That trail was later dubbed the Paris-Vandalia Road. That part of the Paris-Vandalia Road leads from Grandview through the Gap to the Edgar-Coles line, thence to Hitesville, the town that was later mounted on skids and literally dragged by oxen four and a half miles across the prairie to Midway, where the railroad had come through. The railroad passed several miles north of Grandview and Hitesville and changed life along the Vandalia Road forever. This road is today known as the Coach Road. The condition of the trail today is nowhere near as treacherous as it was years ago. Then, after a significant rainfall, the only means of travel was shanks pony. Horses and oxen could not navigate the mud. Today, depending on what township you are passing through, the roads are either oil and chip or gravel. Not so long ago the roads were mud, and this particular trail bragged some very steep hills. Even today there is one ford left that you cannot cross after very heavy rainfall.

From Adin Baber's From Prairie Grass to Cornfield:

> "The freighters dreaded another place, Pitcher's Hill, in now Grandview Township. There was a big gum spring at the foot of the hill. Everyone watered horses there. The freighters usually tried to travel in pairs or trains in order to double up their four and six horse teams to pull the loads up the hill.

> "One freighter had cook stoves as part of the load. These were primitive, formed of sheet iron and made in Cincinnati. The horses stalled on Pitcher's Hill; there was no help in sight, so some of the stoves were unloaded and the part load hauled to the hilltop. The contemplation of all this double work was a wearisome worry to the freighter; he hit upon a solution. The unloaded stoves were on a hillside and leaning precariously, He was a large man; he got down on his knees below a stove and had a helper(the helper, it is believed was Baber's Grandfather) push the stove onto his back. Then, with a mighty heave, he got up and carried the stove and the rest of the stoves up the hill and reloaded them. This was such a mighty feat that it was related for years."

Adin Baber also alluded to a grave site at Pitcher's Hill. Julie Gross, who lives nearby and frequents the surrounding woods and bottoms, knows the area well but does not recollect ever seeing any grave markers in the area or where the old spring would have been.

There are unmarked graves all along the old trace, and of course, many graveyards are still in existence, small family plots, or plots that contain the bodies of settlers who died along the trail. But that is yet another story. History abounds over this south county trace. When one travels over it today, if he travels slowly and carefully scrutinizes the areas as he passes through them, he cannot help but ask himself how exactly those early pioneers accomplished as much as they did.

Steve Stark lives just over the Edgar-Coles County line at Hitesville, on the old trail, just east of the memorial marker that witnesses to the fact that Abe Lincoln traveled over this very road when he was an Eighth Judicial Circuit rider between 1847 and 1849. Steve's father-in-law, Monte Checkley, is as interested in the Civil War era as this writer is of the general history of Edgar County. On a visit with Steve and him, we discussed this article and their immediate relation to it. Monte made the comment that he often tells his granddaughters as they sit on their front porch to just close their eyes and imagine, listen closely, for the sound of horses' hooves and the rumbling of the stagecoach as it comes downgrade toward Edgar County and passes in front of the house. Romantics, he and I; while roaming that trace, it seems that spirits followed me and were saying, "Listen to us, our tales are on the wind."

And so, one can come to several conclusions. The ancient trails that led into Edgar County led to or from the Blackhawk Park area. That area bragged a large encampment of Indians for many, many years and was a major meeting ground for the surrounding tribes. Those tribes were camped at various points along the Wabash River, at the Gap in southwest Edgar County, and at Hickory Grove in the northwest part of the county. There were smaller Indian camps at various places in Edgar County that are also documented but not mentioned in this article.

The Fort Clark-Wabash River Trace was, in all likelihood, a buffalo trace. The trail runs from southeast to northwest. Buffalo migrated from the southeast to the northwest, and Edgar County was home to the bison in early times. The other two major trails, which the buffalo also likely meandered over, were more likely small-game trails utilized by the Indians and earlier man. Those trails connected watering holes, salt licks, good winter cover, and sources of food that only the forest could provide to sustain man and beast. And, of course, the Indians camped and the white man later settled where those commodities could be found. There were many smaller trails, too numerous to mention. They were the shortcuts between the major trails or escape routes used by game and man in time of danger. Even today, in the southern half of Edgar County, one can find roads with more crooks in them than the county jail. These are the remnants of many of the original, lesser trails, trails that the surveyors could not straighten because of geological hurdles such as cliffs, large boulders, and deep ravines.

In virtually any field that one may wander, any field that skirts the Grand Prairie, or any field on high ground on the prairie itself, if one is patient and searches slowly, it is possible he will find an Indian artifact. Searching for those treasures is a pleasant way to spend a spring day. And when one does pick up that arrowhead, he should remember this: he is the first person that has handled that relic in hundreds or thousands of years.

This spring, while you are mushrooming or just strolling one of the ancient trails, take a moment to reflect. Imagine yourself on the old trace two hundred years ago. Are you hunting for food or a spot to settle? And what is that on that large limb overhanging the trail, just above your head and about to pounce?

TRAILS END

OF COURSE, IN THE END, a historian is a re-recorder of events that are known to have happened. Accounts of those events may have been previously written down or passed down the ages by word of mouth to be verified and written down at a later date by the historian. Some of the information in this article was easily gleaned from commonly known sources. Other information came from obscure, difficult to find sources. For example, at one time, I had three different people in three states searching for ancient maps. They found some very old maps of the Illinois land for me.

The story took the better part of two years to research. Eight months were totally lost when this scribe "burned out": information unavailable, two plus two equaled seven, that sort of thing.

I made many new friends and became reacquainted with older friends. One, Asa Baber, an editor at Playboy magazine and a very good writer in his own right, is one who understands the tribulations a writer can experience and also understands what the right word of encouragement can mean to a writer. He gave me the jump-start I needed last November to complete this work.

Here is the list of contributors to this article, and a bibliography is on file at the Edgar County Genealogical Library. Happy trails ...

Adin Baber
Fenton Bottom
Joyce Brown
Jane Campbell, Vincennes State Historical Society
Barbara Carney, Vigo County Historical Society
Doug Cary
Linda Cary, Edgar County Historical Society
Monte Checkley
George Heerman, Illinois State Library
Robert "Jerry" Heltsley
John Hoffman, Illinois Historical Survey
Jenny Johnson, Graduate Library University of Illinois
Walter Kimble
Terry Laughlin
Brenda Lilley
David Lewis, Vigo County Public Library
Lloyd Lewis
Nancy Baber McNeill

Thomas D. Neal
J. T. Penman, ITARP, University of Illinois
Wayne Pinnell
Robert Randolph
Nancy Hogan Reed
Arlyn Sherwood, Illinois State Library—Maps
Nancy Sherrill, Vigo County Genealogical Librarian
Calvin Smith
Robert Steven Stark
Chris Sunkel
Rosie Smith
Kate Swan, University of Illinois Graduate Library
Wayne Temple, PhD, Illinois State Archives
James Trogdon
Rosalee Wirey
And, of course, my pretty proofreader

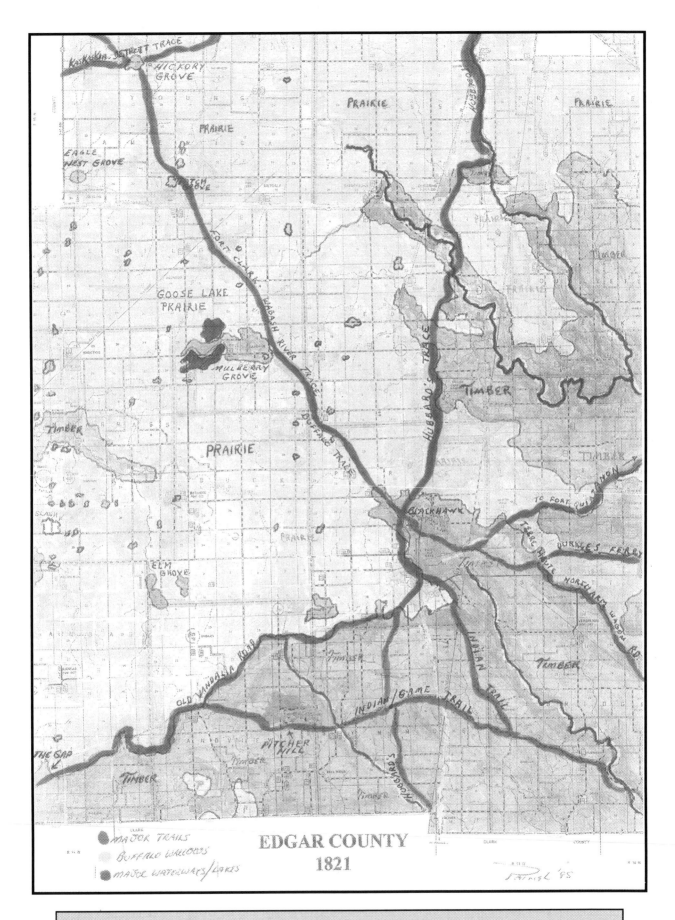

EDGAR COUNTY
1821

THE MAP

THE MAP WAS DONE IN watercolor over an existing map published by the state of Illinois. The locations of prairie, forest, and ponds are taken from the original 1821 survey and field notes of the county. You will notice that the ponds or buffalo wallows seem to be in straight lines. Surveyors were paid by the mile and seldom deviated from their azimuth unless a prominent geological feature dictated that they do so. There were hundreds more ponds and sloughs in Edgar County than are shown on this map. For historical accuracy, if the field notes did not place a pond, neither did I. Most of the groves that are recorded on this map have long ago disappeared because of tiling and tillage. A few were still in existence as late as 1870. Goose Lake Prairie, which was located in the Garland to Hume area, was still mapped in 1870, and today there is still a small acreage remaining of the swamp that has escaped tiling and tillage.

Evidently the goose was in his heyday in the eighteenth and nineteenth centuries. In my research, I found areas designated Goose Lake and Goose Lake Prairie in most of the surrounding counties, and in Iowa and Indiana.

Blackhawk Park is the general area in which the Kickapoo camped. It is also known as the Boy Scout Woods. I refer to that Indian campground as Blackhawk, because by that name, it can easily be found today. There was no other ancient or Indian name given to the area that I could find.

SMITHSON'S CABIN

RECENTLY, WHILE DOING RESEARCH ON old stagecoach stops and the early trails our forefathers trekked to arrive in Edgar County, then the Northwest Territory, I accidentally stumbled upon a log home that was built in 1866. Until just recently, the log home was inhabited, although by today's outward appearances, one would never have guessed what the clapboard siding secreted.

The log home was owned by Ransom and Esther Smithson and was located just east of the Elbridge Townhouse in Southeastern Edgar County. It was rumored that the house had been used as a stagecoach stop in the 1800s, but when I interviewed the Smithsons, they told me they were not sure of the home's role as a coach stop. When I first contacted the Smithsons, Mrs. Smithson advised me that if I wanted to see the log home I had better hurry. The log home was being dismantled, log by log, by Mr. Chester Wallace, a retired contractor, who is relocating the structure to Centenary, Indiana.

One problem writing and researching historical data is that my sources seem to diminish day by day, creating a great urgency. I find myself in a never-ending rush to interview various elderly people, to reap the facts only they know because they lived and experienced the past. What seems to my elders as trivia is my gold mine. And so, camera and notepad in hand, I rushed to the Smithson home. That interview led to others. Days turned into weeks, and at last I can submit the following.

The log home was built between March and October 1866 by Jesse Trout on 39.10 acres that he had purchased from the Edwards family of Champaign County, Illinois, on December 30, 1857. The original land grant was issued to William Edwards on December 4, 1838.

The cabin was constructed of native poplar indigenous to the virgin hardwood forests that covered the area's rolling hills. The logs used were huge, and although there is no record of whom they might have been, Mr. Trout would likely have had to have help felling the trees and dragging the large logs. There were several families homesteading the area, and Elbridge had already been platted by James Ray in August of 1836. Once the logs were dragged to the building site, they were hand-hewn using a broad ax and foot adz.

Here a contradiction arises. Mr. Trout likely needed to be settled in his new home by the coming winter. To save time, the logs were not completely shaved of their bark. Because of this, for the next few springs and summers, the lady of the house would be constantly dusting and sweeping up a very fine sawdust created by wood wasps. The wasps were no threat to man. They were too small to sting; however, the sap from the unseasoned logs drew them like magnets. The wasps would bore small holes in the logs and lay their eggs. The young, when they hatched, would feed on the sap and bark until they reached adulthood, when the cycle would start all over again. This inconvenience would occur until the logs completely dried.However, when it came to notching, instead of using the quicker hog pen notch or the saddle notch, Mr. Trout chose the t notch, and although cutting, "It's is not as time consuming as dovetailing", the "t's" take much longer to cut than the first two mentioned. The notch Trout used was common in Tennessee and Kentucky. It may have been the only method he knew, and he did not know what a voracious feeder the wood wasp is.Once the walls and the roof were in place, the chinking began. The chips from the hewn logs were used as fill between the logs and were held in place by clay mud. One method of mixing mud included the use of hog or horse hair, but in this particular cabin, there was no evidence of either. Chinking was an annual chore. When the clay dried it shrank and was in constant need of patching.

When Mr.Trout began building the house, his youngest daughter was two years old. Over the next decade, his wife would give birth to five more daughters. Although the house was large for this era, 648 square feet, it is difficult to imagine how life would be for eight people living in that small cabin. Trout had built the cabin with thought of adding an upstairs, which in later years he did.

Virginia Chew Maesch's aunt, Hazel Chew Volkers, would relate stories to her of an Indian encampment just south of the log home as late as 1888. Another aunt, Jessie Y. Trout, could recall at one time in the late 1800s, there was an orchard that contained thirty-three apple trees, seven pear trees, several plums and seven grape arbors.

Down the road, just east of the Trout cabin, stands yet today another log home, although it is well disguised. The exact building date cannot be determined. By the size of the logs and style of the cabin, I would place it in the 1850–1870 eras. The cabin is located on land granted to James Ewing on May 22, 1833. Mr. and Mrs. Wayne Goodman reside in the home today. The builder of this cabin, unlike Jesse Trout, was blessed with the luxury of time. The logs are large and uniform in size. He chose poplar and black walnut logs, which once cut, were allowed to dry. The cabin is a full two stories. Instead of the faster notching methods, this builder used the "dovetail notch" itself a thing of great craftsmanship and beauty. This cabin also had hardwood plank floors.

One hears it said time and again, "I wish I could go back!" But really? If one considers the hardships those early Edgar County settlers endured just living and trying to rear children from a wagon or lean-to, smoky fires, laundry in the crick , insects, sickness—no doctor within a day's walk if you were lucky, the massive job of felling and lugging those huge trees ... really?

So this Thanksgiving, while enjoying the turkey you did not have to butcher or bake in an oven that require keeping a bed of coals just so to cook over, pause and reflect on the past a moment and say a special thanks to your ancestors who endured those hardships so you can enjoy the luxuries we have today. I imagine Jesse and Mary Ellen Trout and their daughters had a wonderful Thanksgiving in their new home 131 years ago this weekend.

THANKS FOR YOUR HELP
Ransom B. and Esther Smithson
Mrs. Eli (Joyce) Brown
Mrs. Virginia Maesch
Julie Goodman Garver
Frieda Young
Wayne and Edith Goodman
Thos. D. Neal
Mary Jane Balsis

CHRISTMAS PAST

In October of 1866, the United States was recovering from the tragedies of the Civil War and the assassination of President Lincoln the year before. Reconstruction of the South was in full swing. In the heart of a still young Edgar County, the construction of one of the area's first brick homes was nearing completion.

The Bennett Redmon family had migrated to Edgar County in the 1830s from Kentucky. In 1838, Bennett and his wife, Mary, settled in Symmes Township. Their family consisted of three sons and two daughters. Bennett was a farmer and property owner and sold timber from his land holdings for the building of some of the first corduroy roads in the county. Smallwood, one of Bennett Redmon's sons, married Barbara Perisho in 1862 and, like his father, was a farmer and active in agribusiness. In 1864, the couple presented Bennett with his first granddaughter, Oather Redmon. Whether or not as a celebration of Oather's birth or simply as a grand gesture, Bennett Redmon contracted William Slanker to build the finest house in the county for his son's family.

The date that the house was started is uncertain. As previously stated, it was near completion in late 1866, and it would certainly have taken Slanker and his carpenter, David D. Fisher, more than a year to complete due to the complexity and size of the edifice. The construction was brick, handmade on the site. The framework was of oak and walnut indigenous to the immediate area. The bricks were handmade and stacked in a corbel arch formation called a cove. Firewood was then placed inside the cove and set ablaze. The fires, constantly tended, would burn for weeks. Later, when the fires had cooled and the ashes removed, the bricks nearest the fire were selected to be used for the outside of the house because they were the hardest. The bricks farthest from the fire were softer and were used for the interior walls. Sand and lime were used for mortar. Cement was not introduced until the early 1900s. The inside trim was imported fir, another sign of the Redmon family's wealth.

The house was a two-story structure described in today's architectural circles as a classic Greek Revival I house. The first floor consisted of a great parlor, a parlor, a dining room, and a kitchen. A staircase and hall divided the two parlors. The second-story rooms were sleeping chambers, and they mirrored the first-floor rooms. Both stories had fireplaces in each room, with built-in closets adjoining each fireplace. Although there is no written record of the exact date Smallwood Redmon took possession of the dwelling, by tracing certain events in the construction of the house, it is likely the Redmon family celebrated their first Christmas there in 1866.

By late October of that year, Barbara Redmon was probably engaged in furnishing her new home. Each of the four bedrooms contained washstands, various chairs, and beds. The bed in the master bed chamber, likely a show piece, was valued at one hundred dollars. The furnishings in the parlors consisted of parlor chairs, a rocking chair, sofa, various tables, and bureaus. The kitchen had built-in cabinets on the south wall as well as a built-in closet adjoining the fireplace. It was a large eat-in kitchen, containing a breakfast table and a kitchen table with eleven chairs. In the winter, most meals would have been served in the kitchen because of the warmth radiating from the kitchen range and the fireplace. The cabinets contained crocks and pans, canned fruit and vegetables, and canned meats. Mrs. Redmon had at her disposal cured bacon, canned and salt-cured pickles, and other seasonings and sundries.

The information in this essay to this point is historically accurate. The description of the house was obtained from a paper written by several Eastern Illinois University students in 1998. The furnishings of the dwelling and livestock inventory are listed in Smallwood Redmon's Appraiser's Bill. And although there is no written document describing exactly how the Redmon family celebrated Christmas in 1866, by research we can piece together a likely scenario. And so …

During Christmas week 1866, Mexico was near revolt against Maxmillian. Canada was in turmoil. Lard was eleven cents a pound. Green shoulders and hams were five cents a pound, and sorghum molasses sold for fifty cents a gallon. There were gifts galore to choose from in stores in Paris and Terre Haute. There are no surviving copies of the local Paris paper from the year 1866, but the Christmas ads in the Daily Wabash Express on Christmas Eve that year were plentiful. Brokaw Bros. and Company advertised rocking horses for boys and girls, as well as sleds and toy furniture. Bouche and Co. bragged on imported clarets, bordeaux, and champagne by the barrel. Cornelius and Haggertys offered fine silks, taffetas, and merino wool by the bolt. Edsall and Co. sold ermine, mink, and squirrel coats. Phalon and Sons-New York offered perfumes for the handkerchief—their newest fragrance, Night Blooming Cereus. Brokaw Brothers had the real Santa Claus, and he did not disappear on Christmas Eve but was on hand until January first to give his wee visitors a piece of hard candy. Much like today, the week before Christmas was a busy time. The house needed cleaned and dusted; furniture and silver polished. Egg noodles made and pies were baked … fruit pies from dried apples and plums. Perhaps a mince meat pie made from the scraps of meat and fruit that had been self-seasoning in crocks over the last several weeks. The best potatoes from the root cellar were selected as well as the vegetables that had been canned the past summer. And the goose? That was Smallwood's chore. Pick the fattest of the flock, butcher, pick, and hang him until early Christmas morn.

The Christmas tree was selected and put up Christmas Eve day. The decorations were handmade bows and soft ornaments sewn by Barbara on her newly acquired sewing machine. Strings of popcorn, dried apples, and delicate store-bought glass ornaments also adorned the tree. Candles on the tree were lit briefly on Christmas Eve and Christmas morning. There were gifts to wrap. Oather's gifts may have included a store-bought china doll, a rocking horse, perhaps a handmade corn husk, dried apple doll, and handmade clothes, blankets, and mittens from handspun wool.

After the chores were done on Christmas Eve, and after a light meal, the family retired to the grand parlor. They lit the candles on the tree and hung their stockings from the mantle. Then, by the light of the fire and the kerosene lamps, they listened as Smallwood opened his Bible and read from Luke, chapter two, the Christmas story. Shortly thereafter, Barbara carried Oather up the stairs to her bedstead, tucked her in, and read Clement Clarke Moore's, The Night Before Christmas. And listening to her mother's voice, Oather drifted off to sleep, "with visions of sugar plums …."

Well before sunup Christmas morning Smallwood and Barbara would be hard at work. For Smallwood, the chores included bringing the fires to life, chopping wood, carrying in water for the kitchen range, and stacking firewood by each fireplace. He probably had to dump the chamber pots. His herds consist of twenty-eight head of cattle, twenty-one head of swine, eleven horses, four pair of mules, two jackasses, twenty-seven head of sheep, and the usual complement of barnyard foul. They all had to be fed. He had at least one cow to milk twice a day. Most of the aforementioned chores were done by lantern light. Barbara's chores, though not as strenuous, were equally numerous. She cleaned the thunder mugs and lamp chimneys and brought the range to full heat so Mr. Goose could be put into the oven as early as possible. She played Santa, setting out the gifts and stuffing the stockings. The table had to be set for the family coming for dinner in the new house. She would begin preparing dinner, and sometime in the middle of all these chores, she prepared breakfast for herself, Smallwood, and Oather. While the goose cooked, Oather awakened to find that indeed Santa had visited. Sitting beside the lit tree, the family opened their gifts in turn. Smallwood got a set of brass hames for his prize mules; Barbara a handmade quilt from one of the relatives and a new breakfast shawl.

By mid-morning the family and other guests began to arrive. They brought gifts for Oather and food to add to the already bountiful menu. The men gathered in the parlor to discuss the events of the times while waiting for the Christmas dinner the ladies were busily preparing to serve.

The dinner was grand indeed. There was roast goose, mashed potatoes with giblet gravy, green beans laced with sugar-cured bacon, cinnamon squash, fresh-baked bread and freshly churned butter, fried corn, and oysters fresh from the coast. There were deserts aplenty: mincemeat, apple, and plum pies; date pudding, and hickory nut cake served with white sauce.

At the end of the meal, before the guests harnessed their horses and hitched to their buckboards to hurry home for evening chores, a toast was made to the season with homemade apple brandy. And with this toast, Barbara Redmon would give her family the greatest Christmas gift ever ... her announcement that she was carrying their second child.

This visit to a Christmas past is historically factual. The Christmas Eve scenario is accurate, although there is no written documentation that the events I describe actually happened. Barbara Redmon presented her family with their second daughter, Elizabeth (Bessie) the following year. Smallwood Redmon died three years later, on March 29, 1869, at age forty-nine. There is no known record of the cause of his early demise. The Edgar County Courthouse began recording death certificates in 1870.

The descriptions of the house and its inventory were taken from a paper written by Julie Breu, Jane Carr, Karen Franklin, Kim Snyder, Lori Tussey, and Brent Wielt. They were part of the Historical Administration class at Eastern Illinois University from 1997 to 1998. Their research was, in part, an effort to have the house listed on the National Register. The entire paper can be read at the Edgar County Genealogical Library. Special thanks to Brent Wielt for supplying this special document for my use.

The house described is now owned by Andy and Cyndi Patrick and is known today as Andrew's At The Westbrook, a renowned gourmet restaurant.

My thanks to: Cyndi and Andy Patrick
Jean Waggoner
Gloria Mitchell
Bill Heyduck
The Edgar County Genealogical Library staff
Chris Sunkel
and especially, my pretty proofreader

THE GROCERS

MANKIND HAS BEEN IN THE search of food since the beginning of time. Today, we still have one thing in common with the early caveman: he had to eat in order to survive, and modern technology has not yet relieved us of that same need. Modern technology has given us a more convenient method of obtaining food than running off to the woods and clubbing our supper like our early ancestors were likely to do. Sometimes while shopping for the holidays or stocking up before a big snowstorm, we might feel as if clubbing the ingredients in field or forest would be easier than fighting the crowds in the grocery store.

Early caveman obtained his food on a day-to-day basis. Later, someone figured out that if he obtained a bit more than he himself needed, he could trade his extra staples to his neighbor in return for something he was lacking. You can figure out the rest of that story. The result, of course, is the grocery store as we know it today, and what this article will attempt to do is take you back to a simpler time to follow the evolution of the grocery stores in Paris.

In 1899, the population of Paris was 7,700. The town supported twenty-six grocery stores. In 1961, the town's population was 12,000, but in that sixty-two year time span the number of family-owned grocery stores had dwindled to only four. In 1940, the town was supporting forty-eight thriving corner stores.

Technology and progress were the cause of the demise of the Mom-and-Pop grocery operations that thrived from 1900 to the present. In the early 1900s, the horse and buggy was the primary means of transportation. It was inconvenient to hitch up old Dobbin to run to the store every day. Today, it is no problem at all to jump in the car and run to the store for a quart of milk or a dozen eggs. Because of that lack of convenient transportation, the corner grocery store came into existence, serving a ready-made customer base. If Mom needed two eggs to finish a cake and she didn't have a backyard chicken coop full of laying hens, which many families had at that time, she could send Johnny to the corner store for the two eggs or a stick of butter or whatever. Try going to the supermarket today to buy two eggs or a stick of butter.

In 1899, eighteen of the twenty-six grocery stores in Paris were located within two blocks of the square. By 1930, the number of stores had grown to forty-five, two-thirds of which were located throughout the neighborhoods of the city. This fact seems contradictory in that by 1930, the automobile was beginning to play a major role in people's lives. It was becoming easier to get from one place to another. Two-car families were two decades away, however, and usually when the lady of the house needed something from the store, now was better than later, so the proliferation of the corner stores ensued. Indeed, in 1940 alone, there were forty-eight grocery stores, most of which were Mom-and-Pop operations located conveniently in every neighborhood in the city.

Corner grocery is a misnomer. More correctly, they were neighborhood grocery stores. Between 1940 and 1950, Paris supported over forty of them. All of the stores merchandised fresh produce, dairy products, fresh meat, and poultry. The dairy products were supplied by local dairymen Ed Perisho, Ira Jones, the Heischmit brothers, Frank Huffman, and the Meadow Gold Dairy. These dairymen had regular routes throughout the city on which they delivered fresh cream and milk daily to individual households, as well as to the stores. After the lady of the household arose from bed and dressed, the first thing she would do was open the front door to retrieve the morning's delivery of milk and cream. Before going back into the house, she would remove the cardboard top from the half pint cream bottle and pour some into the cat's saucer; and because of that daily ration of pure cream, the cat probably never cared to catch a mouse in his entire life.

Poultry was supplied by local farmers or the Wadley Poultry Company. Wadley was a New York–based company that shipped fresh poultry daily from area poultry houses. Paris's Wadley warehouse was located on Union Street, between Main and Buena Vista, and had its own rail siding. The local manager was O. C. "Dick" Airhart. The refrigerated cars were spotted and unloaded. Wadley would then deliver the "New York–dressed" fryers to whoever had placed an order on that particular day. The fryers were packed in barrels of ice. "New York–dressed" was the term used to describe the way the chickens were shipped. The birds were shipped ungutted, with their heads and feet still attached. They were delivered to the grocer in that condition. When the grocer took delivery, he would wash the chickens with Ivory soap to remove the waxy residue left from the plucking of the bird. He would then remove the feet and heads and gut the chickens and wash them again before placing them in the meat case. Most of the baking hens were purchased locally from local farmers. When one purchased a fat hen, included with the usual haslettes were extra fat to season the broth and the unlaid eggs that the hen might still be carrying when she met the ax. My grandmother, Ruth Parrish, would stew the eggs with the hen and serve them on the side, with mashed potatoes or noodles or sometimes both. The eggs were only one bite, and they had a flavor that cannot be duplicated today. There was also a market for the chicken feet, which could be prepared in a variety of ways; deep frying was the most common. Some say they are delicious.

The grocers bought most of their eggs locally from area farmers. Canned foods and hardware items were purchased from A. Frey and Son locally or from Hulman Company, based out of Terre Haute, Indiana. Both companies made daily deliveries.

Biscuits, crackers, and cookies were supplied by the National Biscuit Company and the Sunshine Biscuit Company. Phil Sullivan was the local sales representative for Nabisco. Phil called on each of the fifty stores in Paris from 1948 until 1953 on a weekly basis. He remembers his big-ticket items were Oreo cookies and Premium Crackers.

Harold Mathis sold meat, both canned and fresh, for the Swift Packing Company. It would take him three days each week to call on all of the grocers in Paris.

"Cookie" VanDyke sold for the Sunshine Biscuit Company. He called on several local grocers in the forties and fifties. During the summer months, he would often bring along his two sons, Dick and Jerry, now of Hollywood fame.

Fresh meat was supplied by both the Steidl Brothers Packing House and Edgar County Locker Plant. When meat was rationed during WWII, the local grocers were forced to buy their meat from whomever they could. Several went out of town to independent home killers who covertly butchered on their farms. These packers were unlicensed; therefore, the meat was not inspected. But in those days, if one wanted hamburger or steaks, he knew better than to ask where the meat came from. He bought it, took it home, cooked it, and trusted the local grocer, because he knew the grocer's family was eating from the same side of meat.

As you can see, perishable foods were delivered on a daily basis. Keep in mind, in the twenties and thirties, refrigeration as we know it today was still in its infancy, still on the drawing board, so to speak. Folks used "iceboxes" in their homes, a term still used today instead of frig by those of us growing a little long in the tooth. Ice was delivered to each home on a regular basis by horse and wagon and later by motorized truck. The ice man would deliver the ice and place it in the icebox; the blocks were much too heavy for the average housewife to handle. Rambos' Bayou is named after Harry and Ray Rambo. They had an icehouse just south of that finger of Twin Lakes in which they stored ice that had been cut from the lake and a small pond south of the lake.

In 1899, twenty-six grocery stores existed in Paris. Three of those groceries endured until mid-century.

D. D. Anthony hailed from New York State. His grocery career in Paris began in 1893 at 240 West Court. A few years later he was joined by his son, Will. They managed the store together until 1933.

Like all of the stores of that era, many grocery items were shipped in barrels and crates. The customers would measure out a pound of sugar or flour, or hand pick crackers or cookies from the various crates and barrels that lined the aisles.

The Anthonys provided home delivery of groceries, as most grocers did at that time, by horse and wagon. Old Dick, a bay gelding, pulled the load for the Anthonys and was driven by teamster Ollie Clesson. As his daily load lightened, Old Dick would step up his pace, and by the time the last sack of groceries was delivered, the horse would be near full pace, heading for the stable and his own daily ration of groceries.

In 1933, D. D. and Will split the business. D. D. opened a store on North Jefferson, and Will moved his part of the operation to 109 Jasper. The store that Will took over had been previously owned by Ed Feutz, who had opened in the early thirties. The store on Jasper had a stamped tin ceiling, oiled floors, and a pot-bellied stove, around which farmers and friends would gather daily to swap stories and the news of the day. The store also had the familiar candy case from which children, on their way to and from school, could choose their penny candies. The candies were displayed in bulk and consisted of jawbreakers, bubble gum, licorice sticks, and flavored chewing wax. How many of you remember the Planters Peanut man jar, or reaching into the ice water–cooled pop coolers for a nickel Coke or grape Nehi? The seventy-year family business closed in 1960. Three years later, on December 16, 1963, Will and his wife, Minta Ross Anthony died, within three hours of each other.

In 1905, Alfonso Frey bought a grocery store from Frank and Hiram Brubaker located at 213 W. Wood. The Brubaker brothers had been in business since the mid-1800s, and Mr. Frey operated that store until 1918. At that time, Mr. Frey moved the operation to 119 E. Wood and started the wholesale business of A. Frey and Son. When the wholesale operation began in 1918, the automobile era was just emerging. Frey's grocery was, in fact, the first store in the area to deliver groceries by motorized vehicle. For years, the railroads had been the only method of shipping bulk goods, but after W W II, the trucking industry was beginning to make a large impact on the shipping methods.

Carroll Riggs joined Frey's in 1940. He drove one of the large delivery trucks on a daily delivery route throughout eastern Illinois and western Indiana. On a typical day, Mr. Riggs would make deliveries to over one hundred grocery stores. Another of his duties was to drive to the Meade Johnson barge terminal on the Ohio River at Evansville, Indiana, to pick up sugar. Carroll would leave Paris at seven a.m., drive to the dock and load eighteen tons of sugar, which was packaged in one hundred-pound sacks. He would then return to the warehouse by two p.m. to unload the truck.

The depression of 1929 and the bank moratorium of 1932 forced many of the small grocers to close their doors. To combat the loss of local markets, the Freys opened three retail outlets in Paris. These were known as the Blue Link Stores. One of those stores survived until 1986. That store was purchased from the Freys in 1950 by Reginald and Hazel VanDyke and Bill Glick. Reggie had managed the store for the Freys since its opening in 1930. The Freys had purchased the store from Charlie Black, who had moved here from Indianapolis, where he had operated a grocery and delicatessen across from Union Station. Leo Frey and Reggie had worked together at the A&P, which was located where Broadway Video is today at the corner of Main and Court.

The south-side Blue Link was located on the south side of the square. The building was typical of the era, sporting stamped tin ceilings and oiled floors. Reggie, Hazel, and Bill were fixtures in that store. I don't believe any of them missed a day of work in the thirty-six years they were open. On any given morning, Reggie or Hazel could be found behind the cash register counter working on accounts receivable, sipping on sassafras tea. I can remember going into the store, which I did every day for years to visit, and the aroma of that tea filled the air. Reggie could sell a space heater to an Arab. He would offer you a cup of the tonic, and then when you had finished it, he would casually mention that he just happened to have some of the root for sale. For fifteen cents, you could buy five or six of the four- inch roots. I bought a lot of it over the years, but even with Hazel's coaching, I could never get the concoction to taste right. Bill Glick and Hazel closed the operation in 1986, after Reggie's passing.

During the depression years, A. Frey and Son, like so many of the other successful business ventures of the era, was still doing business on an accounts receivable basis. Accounts at local grocers were on a weekly or monthly pay schedule. Many of the smaller operations were unable to provide that service and were forced to close their doors. The "pay me what you can, when you can" philosophy paid off for the Freys. In the long run, the stores did not lose a dime, and a substantial, loyal customer base resulted. Robert Frey, Leo's son, joined the firm after WW II. The postwar era brought on great changes in the grocery business. The neighborhood groceries were gradually being replaced by the "supermarkets". Larger inventories, greater variety, large parking lots, and self-service were concepts the smaller family grocer could understand but didn't have the cash liquidity to pursue. And so, the fifties saw a steady decline and eventual end of the neighborhood stores.

The Blue Link store located at 130 S. Main was purchased by the Freys from E. C. Pollard in 1930. Mr. Pollard had been in business since 1921. L. E. Bennett managed that location until it sold in 1950. The Blue Link located at 122 N. Main was opened in 1930, and was managed by Richard Boyd. Mr. Boyd had been previously employed as a meat cutter by the Parrish Brothers Grocery. For more information on the Frey family business, I refer you to an in-depth article written by the Beacon News editorial staff dated June 12, 1971. Paris Library can provide reproductions of that article.

In the late 1800s, James Arthur Parrish operated a grocery store on the north side of the square. Art had three sons: Fred, Harry, who was nicknamed Heck, and Edgar. In 1903, Fred and Heck bought out their father and renamed the store Parrish Brothers. The store was located next door to the First National Bank, which is now the Edgar County Bank and Trust. In 1921, they relocated to a larger building a half block to the west. Parrish Brothers was open six days a week, from six a.m. until seven p.m. and eleven p.m. on Saturdays. The store provided daily delivery service. In the twenties, two Dodge, open-sided trucks were driven by Dick Boyd and Nate Dawson. On Saturday, the busiest day of the week for most businesses of that era, the delivery men wouldn't see their day end until past ten p.m. Parrish Brothers also employed four full-time clerks. Prior to 1920, grocery stores did not carry meat items. Butcher shops provided meat, and grocery stores provided all other food items. Around 1920, one of the butcher shops began stocking groceries. In self-defense, the grocers began stocking meat items. Parrish Brothers followed suit and hired Joe Haase as their meat cutter. The store didn't carry New York–dressed chickens. Instead, they bought fryers and hens from local farmers and kept them in a pen of sorts in the rear of the store. When a customer ordered a bird, they would fold the wings in such a manner that they could not come loose, tie the feet, and the chicken was delivered live to the customer. Parrish Brothers made their own peanut butter, mayonnaise, thousand island salad dressing, and sandwich spread; free samples were always available on the counter. Plug tobacco was cut to order, and coffee, freshly ground. Of course, as was the practice of the day, when one paid his weekly or monthly account, he always received a free cigar or small sack of candy. Heck Parrish died in 1929, of pneumonia. Edgar was firmly entrenched in a lucrative insurance career, so in 1930, Fred decided to close the doors.

Albert Carnahan opened a store at 319 N. Jefferson, then moved to 210 E. Edgar, into a store that had been owned by the Carpenter family. The Carnahans remained there until around 1960. Joe Haase bought a store from George Steidl at 123 W. Wood Street. Joe and his son Mike operated various stores through the 1950s. Dick Boyd went to work for A. Frey and Son, managing the North Main Street Blue Link.

Rambos' Meat Market also dates prior to 1899. The market was located at 222 N. Main. Howard Rambo opened the business around the 1800s, and his son Harry joined him after the turn of the century. Harry's son Morris "Bud" Rambo recalls working in the market as he was growing up in the thirties. The floors in the store were oiled and covered with a fine layer of sawdust. Bud's job each day was to rake out the old sawdust and replace it with a clean layer. Harry Rambo's market had no delivery service. On occasion, if an order was not too far from the neighborhood, Harry would have Bud deliver it by bicycle. Harry Rambo's market closed in 1943, after Harry died.

Howard Rambo's younger son, Ray, opened a meat market at 126 W. Court in 1937. That store had previously been owned by W. J. Hunter in 1899, who sold out to W. E. Gibbons in 1921, who sold to A. A. Brubaker in 1930. The market, at the corner of Court and Central, was watched over by a friendly English bulldog named Butch. The store had a display case filled with all sorts of mounted animals that drew much attention. On Saturday nights, when the adults came to shop, one of the rituals was to weigh each child on the large platform scale at the rear of the store. The central Illinois area had some unique colloquialisms. One did the "warshin'" on Mondays and regularly changed the "url" in his car. A fireplace had a "chimley". On one occasion, the sign in the front window of Rambo's market read "fresh orsters". One of Bud's schoolteachers advised him of the spelling error. When Bud, in turn, advised his uncle that he had misspelled oysters, Ray explained he had done it purposely to draw folks' attention. Ray Rambo passed away in the mid-forties; his wife, Helen continued the business until the early fifties, when failing health forced her to retire.

In 1910, Roscoe M. Huffman opened a grocery at 1313 S. Central. In 1930, Minnie Kauffman took the store over and ran it until the mid-thirties. Minnie then relocated for a short time to Marshall Street, north of Jasper. From that location, Minnie moved to 225 Carroll, into a store that Tom Gibbons had opened in 1921. Tom Gibbons relocated to 234 W. Court and took over the Reed Grocery. The Reeds had been at that location since 1899.

In 1936, Mrs. Kauffman moved from Carroll to 501 Douglas. The Carroll street store was sold. In 1949, Don Blair bought the store from Harold Mathis and operated it until 1957, when he sold out to the Beck family. Mr. Mathis also owned a grocery at the corner of Liberty and Jefferson. He bought the store from a Mr. Garrett who had purchased the store from Ed Gillum. Mr. Gillum had purchased the store from Noah Hudson, who had been in business since 1930. Mr. Mathis closed that store when Bridwells' opened at the corner of Jefferson and Court in 1952. Prior to Mr. Gillum's venture on N. Jefferson, he had worked in groceries owned by Willis Johnson, the Trover family, and Kenneth Sizemore. Mrs. Kauffman sold the store at 501 Douglas in 1938 to Sam Swartz. Mr. Swartz sold out to Ted Idleman in 1942; he, in turn, sold out to Coach Ernie Eveland in 1951.

When Coach Eveland bought the store, his wife, Mary, who had been a bookkeeper for Art Pothuisje, now found herself a full-time store clerk and meat cutter. Ernie participated by delivering groceries on Saturday mornings. The first summer that the store was open, Mrs. Eveland wanted to take a week's vacation with her son, Bucky, and daughter, Linda, to visit relatives in Canton, Illinois. The daily operation of the store fell on Ernie's shoulders. The first words out of Ernie's mouth when Mary and the kids returned home were, "We are selling the store." After only a year in business, Ernie sold out to Marion Wright, who had previously run Wrights' East Side Grocery at 805 E. Wood. The East Side had originally been opened by William Cummins in 1930.

Minnie Kauffman and her son-in-law, Everett Star Carpenter, were in the 1930s briefly involved in a grocery-meat market operation located at 1306 S. Central. That store was originated by the Holston family in 1910. In 1921, the Holstons sold to J. R. Ellingwood. In 1924, the Witty family owned the store, and they sold out to Loren Abram in 1930. In 1940, Richard Elam bought the store. In 1941, Mr. Elam sold the store at 1306 to the Anderson family. Mr. Elam then purchased a store at 614 S. Jefferson from Sam Swartz. That building was owned by John Boyer. The store itself dates to 1899. Thomas Jones was the original owner. In 1910, W. A. Zimmerly purchased the business, then in 1921, sold out to O. W. Compton. Mr. Compton sold out to John Mason in the thirties. In December of 1946, Richard Elam sold his store to Albert and Frances Valerine, who had moved here from Clinton, Indiana.

The Valerine family was at this location until 1951. When Mr. Boyer sold the building to the Illinois Cereal Mill, Valerines moved to a larger store one block south. That building was owned by Frank OHair. At that time, Albert was joined in the business by his son Danny and daughter Virginia Harris. The Valerine family was in business until 1959. The mill had bought the building, and the Valerines decided not to reopen.

Just a few blocks north, at the rear of 113 S. Jefferson, John Bierbrauer started a grocery only to discover in a short time that the building was too small. He then built a larger store fronting Jefferson Street that years later was home to the DeWitt-Isley Company.

Louis Carli's father opened a grocery in Clinton, Indiana on N. Ninth Street in 1903. In 1926, Louis and his brother-in-law, John M. Volente, opened their own store in Clinton and operated it until 1938. At that time, Louis and his wife, Louise, moved to 624 Vance Avenue in Paris. The store that they purchased at that location had previously been owned by a Mr. Bedino from Clinton, Indiana. Mr. and Mrs. Carli were the parents of six children; the youngest, Robert was just a year old when they moved to Paris. The building went through major remodeling. To accommodate the large family, a basement was dug and several rooms were added to the small structure. The move was timely. Prior to 1938, there had been two other groceries on Vance Avenue. In 1930, Burl Milburn operated a grocery at 529 Vance, and T. T. Kirby had owned a store at 624. Mr. Kirby relocated to 518 Connelly in 1921, and Mr. Milburn was no longer in business; therefore, the Vance neighborhood was in need of a grocer.

During the meat rationing era, Mr. Carli's daily routine included traveling to the Vietti Meat Packing Company in Clinton, Indiana. Mr. Carli would purchase a whole beef, pack it in the trunk of his 1937 Dodge car, and return home to process the meat while Mrs. Carli tended the store and her six kids. Because of Mr. Carli's ability to obtain fresh meat on a daily basis, the business flourished. Mr. and Mrs. Carli closed the grocery in 1974.

In 1925, Charles Curl opened a grocery at 733 N. Main. Prior to that, Charlie had farmed just west of Paris at Mays Station. After three bad seasons in a row, he decided to give up the farming venture and move his family of five to Paris. As an alternative occupation, Mr. Curl approached H. B. O'Hair about driving one of his oil tankers. Mr. O'Hair had a different idea. He was opening a gasoline filling station at 733 N. Main and believed that groceries might be an incentive to draw customers. Mr. Curl agreed to the venture and the forerunner of Curl's Grocery was established.

As Charles's sons grew up, they helped in the store whenever they could. Then, prior to WW II, Bill Curl started his own store in Marshall, Illinois. When the war began, Bill decided to sell the store in Marshall, and shortly after Pearl Harbor, he and brother Bernie enlisted in the U.S. Marine Corps. Both brothers served in the South Pacific. When the war ended, Bill and Bernie returned to Paris and formed a partnership with their father. In 1948, the trio decided to build a larger, more convenient store across the street at 802 N. Main. The building was built by John

Graham with the same materials that were used in the building of Eveland Gym, which had been built by the Works Progress Administration during the war. Eva May Curl Elledge can remember her dad sitting in front of the old store, watching the new structure going up and commenting that each brick cost five cents. The new Curls' was the first supermarket in Paris and the first market to provide drive-up parking. Twice a week, the grocery would buy fresh fish from the markets in Chicago. The fish were shipped fresh by rail in wooden cases. On the mornings the fish arrived, Jim Dillon, the local Railway Express agent, would open at five a.m. so Bernie Curl and Carmen Moore could pick up the fish, take them to the store, clean them, and have them ready for display by the eight a.m. opening. Three times a week, Bill Curl would arise at five a.m. and drive the panel truck to the Wabash Commission Company on North First Street in Terre Haute, Indiana, to pick up fresh produce. Bill would be back in time for the employees to clean and display those items. In 1953, Charlie Curl passed on. Bill and Bernie bought Charles's share of the business and operated as a partnership until March of 1966, when, because of failing health, Bill sold out to Bernie. Bernie ran the business until July of 1971, when failing health caused him to sell out to William Anthony Curl, Bill's son. Tony was the last of the Curl family to operate the store. He closed in 1985.

In 1942, Clint Bridwell moved from Bedford, Indiana, to Oliver, Illinois. He had been in the grocery business for many years in various towns throughout southern Indiana and opened the smaller store for a less vigorous routine. Clint's sons, Vic and Ken, returned to Edgar County at the end of WW II. During the war, they both served in the U.S. Navy in both theaters of war. Ken served as a hospital corpsman, and Vic served as a cook. When they returned to Paris in 1946, they purchased their first store at the corner of Hunt and Austin Streets from Cecil and Viola Terrell. One year later, they moved their grocery to the corner of West Court and Austin streets. That store had previously been owned by the Trover family, who had purchased it from the original owner, John J. Shea. The Shea store dates back to at least 1899. On January 18, 1952, the Bridwell brothers opened the store at the present location, the corner of West Court and Jefferson. The building was built by Victor's son, Tom Bridwell. The store featured state-of-the-art bar scanners and the first automatic meat wrapping machines in the area. A deli and bakery were also added. The loading dock area was improved. Where once it took half a day to unload a truck, it now only took an hour. Today, the Bridwell store is the only survivor of the neighborhood grocery stores in Paris. That survival is a result of foresight and good management practices. Vic and Ken sold the business to their sons, Robert and Daryl. January 1, 1990.

Not too many years ago, it was often heard that the supermarkets killed the small grocer. Not true. or, at least, not entirely true. The larger groceries, such as A&P, Krogers, and IGA, had been in Paris since the beginning of the century. All three chains had more than one store operating in Paris at one time until the mid-fifties. Krogers' forerunner, by the way, was the Oakley Stores. Their prices were lower because of their power to buy, warehouse, and market large quantities of groceries. A. Frey and Son recognized this phenomenon of large volume buying in the twenties. Then, in the thirties, they opened three stores of their own to move the stock.

But when Henry Ford began mass-marketing the automobile in the twenties, a great change was astir. A short thirty years later, Mom didn't have to walk to the corner grocery; she took the car to do her shopping. In the early fifties, the chain stores recognized this shift in lifestyle and consolidated the smaller stores into the larger supermarkets. As marketing evolved, other practices that were once taken for granted slowly fell by the wayside. In the past, it had been common practice to charge groceries weekly or monthly. Accounts receivable were the bane of many of the smaller grocers. Virtually all of them "carried" customer accounts, and collection problems forced some of the smaller stores to close. The larger chain stores were cash only, and by the late fifties, "on-the-cuff" grocery shopping was nearing extinction. The Bridwell brothers were one of the few stores that operated on a cash-only basis from their beginning, and many of their critics didn't believe they would be in business over ninety days.

Packaging changed. Many of us can remember the wonderful mix of aromas that greeted us as we entered the older stores. The smells of oiled floors, sawdust, spices, and freshly ground coffee are now only memories. The sterile plastic packages now imprison those aromas, and the boring odor of sanitizing and cleaning agents now greets us at the local market.

Ironically, as the automobile gained popularity, home delivery of groceries diminished. The auto replaced the horse, and Mom's access to a second family car replaced the delivery man.

The grocery business was very lucrative from the late 1800s until mid-century. The small grocers were all in all good managers and very frugal. Some of them reared large families and funded many college educations. Later, in the fifties, profit margins began to decline. If one could not do business on a large volume, or if he was restricted by the size of his building or by operating capital, he was swallowed up by those who were not so restricted. In 1906, A. Frey and Son grossed over $26,000.00. In 1906, that was a huge amount of money and a lot of groceries when one considers that a can of corn cost seven cents, sugar was five bits for twenty-five pounds, and flour was three cents a pound. Today, $26000.00 wouldn't stock the meat section in most large supermarkets.

There were well over a hundred families involved in the grocery business this century. The stores were small in the beginning and steadily increased in size as population and technology advanced. Finally, the smaller stores disappeared. Today, in a way, the small stores are reappearing. What small town in the rural U.S.A. can you drive through without seeing a Hucks or Casey General Store? H. B. O'Hair knew the combination of retailing gasoline and groceries would work; he was just sixty years too early.

The majority of Paris's neighborhood groceries are listed on the accompanying map. There are omissions. What little data that was available was obtained through the Edgar County Genealogical

Library, Paris Public Library, and interviews with several individuals who were directly involved in the grocery business during the past sixty years.

You have heard it said many times, "Life was simpler back then." Many of the folks I interviewed are in their eighties; a few were ninety plus. During those queries, the "life was simpler" memory, like cream, came to the top. Agreed: Life then compared to now was simpler, more relaxed. Technology has changed our lifestyle, quickened our pace. But before you "wish I could go back to the good ol' days", remember this. Every day one had to chop and carry in the wood, carry water, carry the thunder-mug to the outhouse and empty it every morning, clean the lamp chimleys … . Of course, the kids did get a free stick of licorice when you paid the weekly grocery bill.

DINING IN PARIS

In 1942, when the United States was battling Germany and Japan, Charlie Brown was very upset with President Roosevelt; so upset it seems, that he decided to close his restaurant at 219 N. Main. Charlie was upset because he could not get the vegetable oil he needed to make his famous mayonnaise. Because of the war, vegetable oil was rationed.

As a direct result of his closing, two things of significance occurred: it put Minnie Crum and Veta Asay out of work. No work, no income. Gramma Crum's solution was to open her own diner at 323 N. Main, The Da-Nite. Veta Asay opened the Del Mar Cafe later in 1952.

The other result: F. D. R. did not care if Charlie Brown closed his restaurant or not. Consequently, six months later, Charlie reopened across the street at 228 N. Main, in a much smaller setting, which the Brown family operated until 1976, when Harry, Charlie's son and heir to the diner, died suddenly. The smaller cafe was acquired from C. L. Hamblin, who operated Caps' sandwich Shop.

Charlie's previous café across the street, which Ernie Stephens built in 1926, provided seating for forty patrons and had been open twenty-four hours a day. The new eatery sat only thirteen people and was open fifteen hours a day. The smaller version must have seemed like deja vu for Charlie; his original diner, which opened in 1920, sat only five people. It was so small that when someone finished eating, the rest of the patrons would have to get up and go outside to let the person out. Charlie's wife, Hattie, would bake the pies at home and carry them to the diner every morning. There was a carryout window on the alley to alleviate crowding, and hamburgers were six for twenty-five cents.

The 1942 edition of Brown's offered an L-shaped lunch counter, which seated thirteen people. Harry and Charlie tended the counter and filled the side orders. Ethel Hanner was the head cook. The menu boasted various sandwiches and included such sides as baked beans, carrot salad, Sy Myers's pies, Hattie's chocolate cake, and, in season, bean soup, potato soup and the Brown's own brand of "brown" chili. One could also order such oddities as fried brains or tongue sandwiches. Yes, children, brains! One of my favorite lunches was a brain sandwich topped with homemade pickle relish, a side of cold baked beans with a thick slice of Bermuda onion, a cold glass of fresh buttermilk, and a slab of Hattie's chocolate cake for dessert. Try to find that offering today, all for under two bucks.

During the summer months, the Browns would close down the uptown facility and move to Twin Lakes Park, where they operated the concessions at the beach. These consisted of an arcade, which offered a variety of entertainment, pinball machines, a small dance floor and jukebox, and the swimming beach. Harry served hamburgers, fries, and chili dogs from an eight-stool lunch counter situated at the west end of the arcade.

Harry and Jean had three daughters, Patsy, Chris, and Barrett, all of whom served a tour of duty both at the park and uptown as soon as they were old enough to reach the counter. When their college years stole them away, Jean took over the girls' duties behind the counter.

On certain summer evenings in the mid-fifties, a young man so inclined could steal away to the near darkness of the inner park and snuggle with his young lady on a hidden park bench. There they would, perhaps, be entertained by the bullfrogs in the nearby bayou harmonizing with the Platters crooning from the arcade jukebox, mixed with the waltzes from the merry-go-round and Bud Witticks' unforgettable voice announcing the next batter up at Laker Stadium, which was situated on the south side of the park, all the while munching from a sack of Jim and Marie Popes hot homemade caramel corn. Harry did not reopen the facility after the drought of 1956. At that time, Ross Wright and his wife took over the park and ran it until it closed permanently in the 1960s. Prior to the Browns, the arcade at the park had been operated by Roy and Fern Coogan. The Coogans were yet another family of restaurateurs who were active in the forties and fifties. Nellie Coogan ran a gas station and diner at 1008 N. Main, across from the Goding Shoe factory until 1942. In 1942, Roy and Fern took over and renamed the diner The Hurry in Cafe. They remained there until 1956, when they sold out to Lloyd Wallace. Lloyd Wallace wasn't new to the food business. He had, in fact, started in 1942. He bought the original Bon Ton at 107 Jasper from Clara Mitchel, who had operated it from at least 1937. The Bon Ton was open twenty-four hours a day, seven days a week. Russ Wilhoit and Nell Quarrels were the night cooks. Nell Quarrel and Ruth Broleen had operated Moms' Cozy Corner next door to the Bon Ton in 1940.

Wallace's Bon Ton was famous for its fried potatoes, so famous that Lloyd had one man, Hoppy Hopkins, in charge of doing nothing but preparing and frying potatoes all day long. The menu varied every day: Tuesday, ham and beans, Wednesday, pork roast and so on.

In 1952, Austin Pool and Jesse Bandy bought the diner, which they later sold to Mary Hetherington and Edith Unseld in 1960. In 1956, Austin Pool opened a new restaurant on east Jasper Street, which was very popular with the area teens. Austin tolerated the youngsters taking up room in his booths in the evenings after the supper hour was over. The teens would visit several times each evening and, during each stop, enjoy a Coke and french fries.

Let's revisit the Wallaces. In 1956, at their new location on North Main, Lloyd and Nila renamed the venture Wallace's Town and Country. They added a large and more formal dining room onto the south side of the building, complete with a large electric organ. On nights when Lloyd could find some breathing room from his many kitchen duties, he would entertain his diners with almost any tune one might request.

The restaurant was open for breakfast, dinner and supper and bragged a wide-ranging menu. Frank Wallace's wife, Flossie, and Lloyd's wife, Nila, were the two principle employees, responsible for virtually every duty that had to be done. Lloyd recalls that Nila wasn't too pleased with the restaurant business. One could understand her misgivings considering that every morning Nila would bake forty-five to fifty pies. And they were delicious; by early supper hour, the pies were usually gone.

The new addition was also used as a meeting room for service clubs or was let for special occasions. I remember the Paris Tiger football squad used to have their Thursday night pre-game banquet there, where we feasted on everything from fried chicken to steak to fish. The meals were large and very good. Then, on a full stomach, the team would have to listen to one of the pillars of the community orate on the next night's game, sportsmanship, it's not how you play the game ... Sadly, the speeches didn't help much. In four years we did not win a game. It wasn't because of the food though; it was delicious. Wallace's Town and Country closed in 1967.

There was one other diner in business within a block of the Wallaces' on N Main, but before it is identified, there is a fact that should be revealed to those who are not familiar with the layout of Paris in the thirties through the fifties.

On North Main, within a half block of one another, were two major industries. The U. O. Colson Company, which occupied the large, two-story building in the 900 block, employed over 200 people in its lithographic printing and advertising specialty business. The other, the Goding Shoe Company, opened in 1926, in the 1000 block and employed 175 people in its peak production years. So there was an opportunity for someone in the food business to capitalize on these large numbers of workers. Although most workers undoubtedly carried their lunches to work, a significant number of them ate dinner every day at one diner or the other.

The other diner of note was Ray's Cafe, which was located immediately north of Colsons. It was owned by Ray and Mabel Smith and was housed in a two-story, glazed tile building. The diner was downstairs; the Smiths lived upstairs. Ray and Mabel, as far as can be determined, began serving meals in 1937 at 233 N. Main and remained there until 1947, when they sold that diner to Oather Adams, who in turn sold the business to Truman Wright in 1949.

In the interim, Ray moved to 913 N. Main to capitalize on those workers who wanted lunchtime meals. I could not verify the exact lunch hours for the two plants, but I do remember that between eleven a.m. and one p.m., it was difficult to find a place to sit at both Ray's and Coogan's. Ray and

Mabel Smith went so far as to pre-set each table. They knew who sat where, what they wanted for dessert, and what beverage they preferred with their meal.

To someone not familiar with the modus operandi, who just happened into the diner before eleven a.m., it must have seemed eerie to see the tables set but no patrons to partake. Of course, when the plants let out for dinner, the eateries filled immediately.

Ray's also served supper in a more tranquil atmosphere. Like most of the restaurants of the era, they served complete, homemade meals as well as sandwiches. The Smiths remained in business until the mid-sixties. They closed after Goding had closed their doors, Colsons had cut back, and their health had begun to fail.

Another prominent name of that era was Rankin. Lee and Della originally began in 1940, in a restaurant they acquired from Abraham and Lillian Wells. The eatery was located at 206 W. Court and dates to 1930. The diner was called the Illinois Cafe, and the Rankins remained there until 1952, when they sold out to Harvey Inman. Inman sold out to Ralph Hale in 1960.

Meanwhile, the Rankins had moved to the corner of North Main and Elliot, directly across from the Goding Shoe Factory, and opened a tearoom. Unlike the Coogans and Smiths, the Rankins catered exclusively to the supper crowd. Their specialty was fried chicken. Lee's chicken recipe was outstanding, and to this day, I have yet to taste anything quite like it, nor have I been able to duplicate it. How many times have you said to yourself, I wish I could cook and get the flavors like Gramma used to? Throughout the years, I have tried to recapture the flavors and tastes of many of my mom's and gramma's recipes, but to little or no avail. Two facts seem to explain why I cannot accomplish this. Neither of them ever used exact measurements, a pinch of this, a pinch of that, and each pinch was as unique as the person doing the pinching. Also, the ingredients were much different. The flour was coarser, the milk was whole, and the chickens were raised on the ground. In the late fifties, the Rankins moved their tearoom to 426 W. Washington. Failing health caused them to close in the early sixties.

Just north of the Big 4 tracks at 323 N. Main, Minnie Crum was doing just fine. As you recall, she was temporarily out of work when Charlie Brown closed in 1942. Minnie's new diner, the Da-Nite, was purchased from Everett Englebright in 1943. He had obtained the restaurant from Bertha Sexton. Mrs. Sexton had been a beautician for many years before her venture into the restaurant business. She apparently discovered the food business was not to her liking, because she traded the diner to Mr. Englebright for a 1941 Ford. "Gramma Crum," as Minnie was affectionately known, was open from four a.m. until nine p.m. She was renowned as a very good cook, and her business reflected that. The Da-Nite menu consisted of the usual entrees that were common to the times. During my later grade-school days as a treat, I was allowed to go to lunch there once or twice a week. My usual lunch was two hamburgers, fries, and a chocolate milk shake. In 1954, that fare cost under one dollar. Of course, as the old-timers said, "That's when a buck was a buck."

Reflecting on that: one Saturday each month, I was allowed to go to the movies at the Lincoln Theater. I would leave early enough to get a haircut at Ray's barbershop at the corner of North Central and the Big 4, then a shoe shine at the parlor next to the Lincoln Theater. I would still have enough money to buy my movie ticket, a box of Milk Duds, and a bag of peanuts that, for some reason, we would pour into our Cokes. That afternoon cost less than six bits.

Just across the street from the Da-Nite was the Shamrock Inn. Pat Murphy was the proprietor, and it dates from 1952 to 1960. Back to Charlie Brown's story. When the Brown's temporarily closed in 1942, as I said, Veta Assay was suddenly unemployed. Not much is known about her activity in the dining-room business until she reappears in 1952 as the owner of the Del Mar Café, which was located at 247 North Main. The café was named after her son. The restaurant dated back to 1947, when Ernie Cunningham operated it. In 1949, Charles Hunter is recorded as the owner, and he in turn sold the enterprise to Mrs. Asay. Mrs. Asay moved the restaurant to the north side of the square, where it remained until the mid-sixties.

Interestingly, on North Main from 1930 to 1960, there are twenty-five different restaurants recorded. The Big Four was situated behind the depot between Main and Central. In 1930, Truss Gilbert was the owner. E. R. Nightlinger took over in 1940 and operated it until it closed in 1956. They catered to the train crews and passengers as well as a local following. In 1930, Grace Roberts served meals at 237 N. Main under the railroad watch tower, until at least 1942. Her establishment was known as the Majestic Cafe. Herbert Seeley, Lola Shanks, F. M. Clawson, C. F. Kelley and Nora Houston are all recorded as being owners of restaurants in this era, but very little information, other than location, is available on any of these people or their ventures. In 1930, Jesse Sanders ran a diner at 214 N. Main. Every noon, Mr. Sanders would stand in front of his diner, sporting a starched, clean, white shirt, light a huge cigar, and for one minute, ring a dinner bell that announced to the surrounding businesses that dinner was ready. Jesse did this until 1942, when the restaurant was acquired by L. E. "Noah" Carpenter. Noah Carpenter had been in business since 1940. He operated Carpenter's Lunch at 145 E. Wood. It was a small luncheonette. When Noah moved to 212 N. Main, he was in a much larger setting and chose a cafeteria format. His specialty was Swiss steak, but he offered a varied selection of meats and a large choice of vegetables, salads, and desserts.

On about any morning, the Beacon News crew and several local merchants would meet there for coffee and donuts to discuss the latest happenings. Among those were Paul Mc fall and Gus Niles, who ran the Paul Mcfall Clothing Store, Chuck Inge ran McCoy's Shoe Store, Paul VanGilder of the Beacon News, Harry Parrish of The Parrish Insurance Agency, and others too numerous to mention.

As we have seen, many of the diners were located on North Main. The majority of them were scattered throughout the city however. One of these that is still in business today, the Paragon Cafe, dates back to 1937 and is located at 108 E. Court. Ethel Miller owned the diner at that time. In 1940, it was operated by Elmer Ress, who named it, appropriately, Ress Taurant. In 1942, Byford Wright, Monte's son (Wrights' Cafe, 253 N. Main, 1930), bought the diner and operated under the names The Friendly Cafe or Wrights Cafe. In 1956, Charlie Grumley bought Wright out and renamed it The Ritz.

Mr. Grumley had been in and out of the restaurant business in Paris since 1940. At that time, he owned the College Inn Restaurant and Dance on North Main. He remained there until 1942, when he moved to the north side of the square and opened The Ritz Sandwich and Soda Grill. Not much information is available about Charlie from 1943 until 1960, when he opened at the Court street address. Charlie's father had been a tailor in Paris, a trade that he passed on to Charlie. I remember that Charlie was in the tailoring business probably during the years he was not involved with the restaurant trade. Charlie also followed the county fair circuit. He had a foot-long hot dog stand that he pulled behind his car. He was one of several individuals from Paris who followed the county fair circuit, but theirs is a story to be told later.

Other cafes not so long lived included Bus Cafe at 131 Court, ran by O. M. Sizemore; Marie's Lunch Room, at 509 W. Washington, by Marie Owens; Runyan's Lunch, 236 N. Main, by Guy Runyan; Dainty Dinette, 132 E. Wood, by Mrs. Guy Simpson; Melody Rendezvous, 813 Springfield, by Earl Wilson; Quality Cafe, 950 N. Main, by Helen Eliot; and The Snappy Service Inn, by L. Knowles.

The Snappy Service Inn should not be confused with the Snappy Service, which many will recall, was located immediately south of the Lincoln Theater. The later was originally known as The Lincoln Grill and was owned by A. W Godin. It apparently closed briefly during the war. In 1952, it was reopened by Russel Finney and later owned by Robert Knowles. The big draw was hamburgers: six for a buck.

The Corner Cupboard was another cafe that benefited from a major industry in Paris. It was on West Court Street, at the intersection of the Big 4 railroad. The Merkle Broom Factory was situated one-half block west. Helen Trover is listed as operating the diner from 1942 through 1960, when Francis Ketner took over. The diner catered to the Merkle lunch trade as well as to the nearby yardmen who tended the trains in Midland railroad yards.

Three major restaurants were located on Jasper, the main east-west artery through Paris. The Del Mar Cafe was located at 103 W. Jasper and was owned by Dale Sexton. The diner can be traced back to 1937. It was a very small diner that specialized in barbecue. The diner also had one of the first carryout windows.

In 1945, when they returned from the war, Bill Anthony and Leon "Cookie" Holcomb purchased the restaurant. They enlarged the building by adding a room on the rear and renamed the restaurant The A and H. The larger diner had four booths, five tables and a fifteen-stool counter. They were open from five a.m. to nine p.m. seven days a week. Leon and Bill rotated days so that one of them was always on duty. The diner featured a full menu with a different main course every day. A meal at that time cost forty-five cents. One of the meals, a favorite of many customers, was their pork chop dinner. Bill and Cookie decided to double the size of the pork chop to get an edge on the nearby competition, which offered basically the same meal for the same price. At the same time, they raised the price of the meal to sixty cents in belief that the patrons would pay the extra fifteen cents for the larger serving. The reaction from their clientele was, "You can get the same meal next door fer forty-five cents". That plan was scrapped.

The A and H's big drawing card was homemade ice cream. Bill and Leon wanted to compete with the Elliots, who operated an ice cream parlor uptown. They found a gentleman from Lawrenceville, Illinois, who had a good recipe and purchased it for five hundred dollars. They made forty gallons of vanilla, chocolate, and peppermint fresh every other day in the back room of the diner. To make the peppermint ice cream, they bought extra large candy canes and crushed them with a large hammer, then mixed it into the ice cream before freezing it. The ice cream freezer itself was not unlike the version folks used in their homes. It used ice and salt, was hand-cranked, but was much larger than the home version. The freezer could produce ten gallons of ice cream, which when finished, would be packed into five-gallon containers and placed into a special refrigeration unit, which would quick freeze the product.

Bill and Leon were in business until 1956. Leon then began a new career with Meco, and Bill moved to Indianapolis to become the supervisor of cafeterias for Ford Motor Company. Both remained in those positions until their retirement.

In 1930, Lawrence Frazier was operating the Illinois Auction Commission Company. It is the oldest-running auction company in the state of Illinois and dates back to 1885. It was designed after an auction company operating in Paris, Kentucky. The auction was, and still is, held every Thursday and enjoyed a large clientele of local livestock producers. To meet the needs of the hungry farmers, Charles and Glenn Barr built a portable lunch wagon, which they sat up in the parking lot each Thursday and from which they served fish sandwiches and coffee. The lunch wagon was utilized until 1945, when the stockyard burned. Lawrence and Ed Frazier rebuilt the yards, and the new building included a diner, which is still in business today. On March 13, 1980, the fiftieth anniversary of the Illinois Auction Commission Company was observed. On that day, the old lunch wagon was revitalized, and Glenn Barr served fish sandwiches and hot coffee once again. The coffee was served in tin cups, which were given away as souvenirs to the patrons that day. In 1946, Glenn Barr returned from the war. The stockyard had its own diner, so Glenn built a restaurant across the street. It was a large, two-story, glazed tile building, which seated sixty diners downstairs. Upstairs there were two apartments and a medium-sized banquet room. The restaurant was open from four a.m. to midnight, seven days a week. On Christmas Day, Glenn would open up by himself to fix sandwiches for those who had nowhere else to eat or for the occasional traveler. The restaurant was also the bus stop for Greyhound, Western Motor, and the Crown Transit Lines. The menu included full dinners and sandwiches. The fish sandwich remained the favorite fare. Glenn also baked his own pies. Inez Blaker was the day cook for many years, and Helen Gleckler cooked from four p.m. to midnight. More interesting reading about Mr. Barr can be found in an article by Perry Piper in Growing Up On Muddy Creek, "Fish Monger Extraordinary".

There were a few lunch counters in Paris that date from the thirties and which should be mentioned. Pearman Pharmacy, which was located on the east side of the square in the location where Eli Lilley began in the early 1900s, had a small lunch counter. They served a very good hot ham salad sandwich. That recipe was used through the sixties until the lunch counter segment of the business was terminated.

The Dorris family operated the Walgreens drugstore on the southeast corner of the square for years. In fact, that particular lunch counter dates from the thirties. The bus stop was located nearby on South Main in the thirties, and the restaurant served full meals.

Wright's Drugstore, directly across from Walgreens, had a small soda fountain and lunch counter, as did Fritches on the west side of the square. Woolworths' Five and Dime also served sandwiches in the fifties and sixties.

Another facet of the restaurant business that should be noted is the dining rooms in the early hotels. There is not much information available on the hotels, but three particularly stand out.

In 1930, on the south side of West Court Street, where the Cairo Line Railroad intersects, there was a hotel operated by Mrs. Pearl Cookson. This building still stands today. For many years after the hotel operation ceased, it was a small tavern. Then, in the early fifties, Don Osborn remodeled and opened a restaurant featuring charcoaled steaks and fried chicken. Don and Katie's was a very popular steakhouse. It featured two large fireplaces, which in the winter were utilized and provided a warm, cozy atmosphere in which to dine. The bar in the front of the building remained the same. There were two dining rooms, one of which served as a family room; the other dining room, in the rear, featured a waterfall, fireplace, and smaller bar to serve that area. The restaurant catered to a far-reaching clientele, and local patrons who frequented the steakhouse were often surprised to see the various dignitaries who had visited Paris that day and were dining there that evening. Some notables were Senator Charles Percy, Governor William G. Stratton, and an array of state senators and congressmen. The restaurant is still in operation today. The Station is operated by Dennis and Dianne Ingram.

Further east on Court, just off the square, was the Hotel France. The hotel had a large, formal dining room as well as a breakfast room. The dining room served as a meeting place for the service clubs and also hosted several conventions that various local companies put on. The dining rooms closed in the fifties but have since been remodeled as close to the original decor as could be determined. It is now operated by the Kensington Corporation.

The Central Hotel was located at 241 N. Central at the Big Four tracks. It dates back to 1864. In 1930, the hotel and restaurant were run by Effa Yates. In 1947, Claude Davidson reopened it as the Ideal Cafe. In 1952, it was known as the Candlelight Cafe, owner unknown. In 1956, Floice Lance was the proprietor. In 1959, L. Don Morris took over. Mr. Morris had operated the Morris House Hotel since 1946. The restaurant he took over had been in continuous operation since 1928. In 1964, Mr. Morris had planned to completely refurbish the grand dining room and hotel, which was a combination of the Grand Central Hotel and the St. Nicholas Hotel.

Apparently, existing laws that dictated the codes under which hotels could be built or remodeled caused the remodeling to be too expensive. Mr. Morris opted to close the doors permanently on June 2, 1964. The Floyd Hegg Motor Company purchased the property, razed the building, and constructed a used car lot, which occupies the spot to this day.

There are many omissions in this article. The information on restaurants prior to 1930 is sketchy to say the least. From 1930 to 1960, there is little information available, that is, names of restaurants, their owners, and where they were located. My information was obtained through city directories and old phone books. Many of the books are missing from the libraries of the Historical Society and the Paris Library itself, therefore gaps exist. There were many restaurants in business less than a year for whatever reason. Therefore, this writing was based on the longevity or the continuity of the more frequently found data. The drive-ins and more faddish diners were omitted purposely, for those are a topic in themselves.

For this article, I interviewed a dozen or so people who were directly involved with or who had firsthand knowledge of those restaurants mentioned. If you have knowledge or memories of the older restaurants, jot them down and send them to the Historical Society. Also, they would appreciate any old city directories or phone books you may have lying around, especially those that date to the turn of the century.

And finally, if there was one thing that stood out the most in the interviews and research, it was the dedication, hard work, and extremely long hours that restaurateurs devote to their avocation. They love their work!

WILLIE

The journal's entry for July 17, 1933, states, "Willie left us this afternoon at 1:30."

But as the king said to Alice in Lewis Carroll's Alice in Wonderland, "Begin at the beginning."

As any auctioneer will tell you, many treasures can be found at estate auctions. When one bids successfully on a box of what, at first glance is nothing but odds and ends, the bidder may be surprised at what turns up in the bottom of the box. The old adage, "One man's junk is another's treasure," more often than not is proven correct. This particular auction treasure, a handwritten journal from 1933, had lain hidden for thirty-two years and was actually discovered twice. The book, a blue hardback, five by seven inches in size, contained three hundred pages for writing. It was specifically designed to be used as a journal or diary and was first found by Edith Cravens Swinford in a box she purchased from the estate sale of Mabel Downing Hurley who, unbeknown to her children, had kept the book secreted until her death on February 22, 1965. The journal was unsigned, and not being able to determine who had authored the book, Mrs. Swinford placed it aside. For thirty-seven years it was left untouched in Edith's garage. In the summer of 2002, Henry Boren rediscovered the journal while he was cleaning out Edith's garage and preparing for her sale. However, this time the book did not sell. Henry's wife, Nancy Cravens Boren, gave the journal to her son-in-law, Tony Haupt, to read; he, in turn, let this scribe read it, and the unraveling of the mystery began.

The puzzle as to the author's identity was not actually that hard to solve. The unsigned journal chronicled events from March until July 1933. Although many of the family names mentioned would be familiar to older residents of Edgar County, and particularly Hunter Township, the author's last name remained a mystery even though he referred to his wife and children by their first names on nearly every page of the book. Upon the first reading of this work, there was no clue that the first names so often mentioned were even related to the author. By studying the families whom he frequently mentioned by last name, it was possible to deduce that the story took place in Hunter Township of Edgar County, Illinois. The author had predated his pages a week in advance. The last four pages had no entries, just that final entry written apparently by his wife. It should be noted here that this journal was likely a work very much appreciated by his wife in that she could bring herself to make that very painful last notation in his journal. With the information from the last entry, this writer went to the Edgar County Clerk's Office and, with Becky Clark's help, looked up the records of death on July 17, 1933, and thereby discovered the author's identity—William Wesley Downing.

The events recorded in the journal center on the daily routine of Mr. Downing's family. Willie had married Mable Dixon, and by 1910, they had settled on twenty-seven acres on the south side of the road immediately east of Baldwinsville in Hunter Township. That year the first of their eight children, a daughter Dorothy, was born. Over the next seventeen years, they would have seven more children, and today, Betty, who was born October 2, 1927, is the only surviving child.

Baldwinsville no longer exists. In fact none of the small towns that were prevalent in Hunter Township in the early 1900s exist any longer. From the history book Our First One Hundred and Fifty Years—Hunter-Stratton-Elbridge Townships, we learn that in the 1800s, Hunter Township boasted, "more villages and hamlets than any other township" in Edgar County. The census of 1870 recorded 1,029 citizens in Hunter Township, but by 1930 that number had dwindled to 895 because of a sequence of events that would forever change how rural business was done.

Much earlier, in 1823, Paris had been designated the county seat. This in itself doomed the town of Cambridge City, which was later known as Baldwinsville. Then, in 1835, the railroads advanced into Edgar County. Prior to the railroads, the small country stores relied on horse-drawn freighters from St. Louis, Chicago, and New Orleans to provide everyday staples—food items, dry goods and hardware. The arrival of the railroad in Paris made shipping and receiving goods simpler and quicker. Thus, Paris could provide a greater variety of shops and services. The proprietor of a small country store in the late 1800s would have begun to see the writing on the wall. If he wanted more business, the move from the country into town was necessary if, for no other reason, than a larger market. The arrival of the automobile provided farmers with a still more flexible and quicker mode of transportation to and from the city. The death knell for the small, country store was peeling. In March of 1933, Perry Martin was still managing one of the last surviving country stores in Edgar County at Baldwinsville.

John Ditto, a butcher who peddled meat, eggs, and butter from a horse-drawn wagon throughout many of the nearby townships had opened a dance hall next door to Martin's store. And just down the road, east a half-a-quarter, Willie Downing, his wife, Mable, and their seven children were going about their normal everyday routines. Normal other than the fact that Willie, who had been a farmhand all his working life, was now bedridden. Willie was suffering from "dropsy."

Dropsy is defined as "an abnormal accumulation of a clear fluid in a body tissue or cavity". In Willie's case, it was debilitating in that it had affected his kidneys and would eventually cause his demise. His death certificate stated he died of "interstitial nephritis" or kidney failure. His life with today's technology, dialysis, and modern medicines, would likely have been prolonged, but remember, this was 1933, when no such technology yet existed. That illness finally forced Willie to bed in March of 1933. The family had placed a bed in the living room of their home, and from that bed for the next five months, Willie observed the daily goings on of his family and noted them in his journal.

The journal gives us a brief glimpse into the life of a farm family during the Great Depression of the 1930s. Although families nationwide were struggling just to make ends meet, "Brother can you spare a dime?" nowhere in his writings did Willie complain about those hard times. The family was evidently self-sufficient and made do with what was at hand. Willie never referred to the lack of money nor did he complain about his illness. His writings were more on a positive note, commenting daily on the weather, his children's activities, various farm chores, and even two items that held the nation's immediate attention—an assassination and the Depression.

On February 25th, Willie wrote: "Mayor Cermack was not expected to live they gave it out over the radio"

In Miami's Bayfront Park, on February 15th, Chicago's mayor, Anton Cermack, had been shot by Guiseppe Zangarra, an Italian immigrant, who believed if he assassinated President-elect Franklin Delano Roosevelt, his stomach pain would go away. The mayor died on March 6th from the gunshot wounds. Twenty-five thousand people attended his funeral on March 10th at Chicago Stadium, and nearly that many more were turned away because of a lack of seating. And while the nation mourned the death of Mayor Cermack, the Depression had its grip on the economy. On March 2nd, he writes: "They stopped paying checks at the bank you couldn't only get five per cent of your money." Two days later he writes, "Wilbur [Frances] said they closed the banks today." And on Friday, March 10th, he noted, "Mayor Cermack was buried today the banks closed tight today."

The March 2nd edition of the Daily Paris Beacon News headlined the banks' restrictions on withdrawals. In a joint meeting of the boards of directors of the Citizens Bank and the Edgar County Bank, this statement was issued: "By recent action taken by banks in nearby states, an unsettled condition has arisen in this locality and our banks have been threatened with unusual withdrawals by persons for hoarding or by persons withdrawing for other than usual or business needs … the banks of Paris have agreed to restrict withdrawals to not more than five per cent of balances as shown at the close of business March 1, 1933." On March 4th, Roosevelt's inauguration day, a national bank "holiday" was declared until March 7th, and F. D. R. addressed the issue in his inaugural speech. Let me assert my firm belief that the only thing we have to fear is fear itself—nameless, unreasoning, unjustified terror which paralyzes needed efforts to convert retreat into advance." On Friday, March 10th, Roosevelt extended the bank holiday until, "further proclamation by the President." In an editorial addressing the moratorium, the Beacon stated that although some areas had been devastated by the Depression, Edgar County had been more fortunate and asked people to be patient and "persevere." But the effects of the Depression were severe to many in the county and devastating to some families. A local family was one of those. On February 20th, Willie had recorded, "A neighbor shot himself with a shotgun on account of no work he was at Blanford."

Closer to home, Willie had a more pressing problem. Willie's father, Frank Downing (m. Aline Hess), was fighting for his life. In February of 1933, Frank Downing's health took a turn for the worse. Then on Monday, March 6th, Willie wrote, "Fay brought eggs for the incubator ovals sow had eight pigs they call oval around ten o'clock tonight and said dad had passed away." William Frank Downing died of a stroke caused by hypertension or high blood pressure. The high blood pressure had occurred because of interstitial nephritis, dropsy, the same illness that plagued Willie. Willie was too sick to attend his father's funeral but described the day in his journal:

> "March 8th Wednesday … it is a nice day but the wind is blowing and it is pretty cool and liz and com [Stafford] come up and took the folks to dads funeral it will be at 2:30 today burial will be in the bethesida cemetery over by liggett jane went to ferry and said mrs ferry would come down and stay with me com and lizzie brought the folks home and oval and fay brought ray mrs ferry genieve paul and donald come down after supper."

Before delving into the journal any further a few explanations are in order. In his journal, Willie wrote in the cursive style. His penmanship is very legible; he had, as they used to say, "a good hand." He used given names but rarely surnames and did not capitalize names. He also seldom used punctuation marks. As this writer quotes from the journal, surnames, when known, are added in brackets.

Willie and Mable had eight children. Only seven were living at the time the journal was written. They were, in order of birth:

Dorothy who was born October 21st, 1910, lived only two days.

Ray and Fay were twins born in 1911. Fay married Oval Tolliver, and they had taken up housekeeping a few miles east of Baldwinsville at the time the journal was written. James Ray served in WWII in the 130th Infantry Division in the Pacific Theater Campaign. He earned the Combat Infantry Badge and two Bronze Stars for the New Guinea and Luzon battles in 1945. He also was awarded a Bronze Star with his Philippine Liberation Ribbon.

Vernon was born October 19, 1913. Died 1944. He served in the Army Air Force as a tail gunner.

William Arthur was born in 1915. He served in Panama during WWII. Several years after he returned home from the war, in 1949, he was killed in an auto accident on old Route 16, west of Paris, on Sharkey's curve.

Charles was born in 1919. He was a second lieutenant in the headquarters division of the 82nd Airborne. He was killed by the Germans after his glider landed at Normandy on D-Day.

Jane was born in 1920.

Betty Neer was born October 2, 1927, and today resides in Spring Lake, Michigan.

Mable Downing was a Four-Star mother as all of her sons were serving in WWII.

Fay, William Arthur, Charles, Mable, and Willie are buried in the Little Grove Cemetery east of Paris on Route 150, just east of the Vermillion Road.

In 1933, Betty would have been preschool age, Jane and Charles were in grade school, William Arthur was likely out of high school, and Fay had married Oval Tolliver. Ray and Vernon were living at home.

The spring of 1933 was wet. But although it rained much of March and April, it did not seem to dampen the daily activities of the Downing family. The boys fished and turtled on Brouillett's Creek and mushroomed along the creek bank. The family hunted mustard and dandelion greens. On April 17th, Mable planted potatoes in the garden that Oval had turned over for her earlier that spring. Later in May, she planted onion sets, radishes, lettuce, and cabbage seed. In March they had started saving milk from their cow. They traded that milk with the neighbors for coffee, sugar, seed potatoes, and eggs. The eggs were incubated in a brooder house. On March 18th, Mabel and Fay had "set eggs," placed them in the incubator. On April 8th, eighty chicks had hatched, and by May 29th, they had successfully hatched 251 chicks, two goslings, and several ducklings. Those chickens would be put to good use. A fat baking hen, one past her prime, sold for sixty cents. The fryers would be sold or traded, and the young layers utilized for yet more eggs to be sold, eaten, or incubated to replenish the depleted flock. In May, Willie noted, "Mabel sold some chickens in town to buy Jane a pair of shoes."

My uncle, Joseph Edgar Parrish, returned from WWII when I was four years old and immediately became one of my favorite uncles. Joe was courting Kathleen Noyes, a lovely lass from Martinsville, Illinois, and on occasion, I was invited to accompany them on dates. In 1948, they were married and took up farmsteading on one of my grandfather Edgar's farms, four miles west of Wetzel Station in Edgar Township.

One of my great pleasures was being allowed to stay weekends with Kathleen and Joe on the farm. They had a milk cow who was very tolerant of a little boy who, no matter how hard he pulled and yanked, could not produce a drop of milk; naturally I was in awe of Uncle Joe who could not only fill the pail but could also nail a cat square in the face—a cat who sat ten feet away, patiently awaiting her evening treat. There were pigs to throw rocks at and a very tolerant Tennessee Walker riding horse who did not at all seem to mind the attentions of a very enthusiastic young man. And, of course, they had a chicken yard.This writer learned three lessons about chickens in that yard. The first lesson was hens did not mind when you reached under them as they sat on their nest to retrieve the morning's eggs if you were very gentle in doing so. The second lesson was every chicken yard had a "boss hog," a chicken not to be messed with. In this particular case it was a Rhode Island Red rooster that had a very mean disposition. My cousin Jimmy had been to the chicken yard with Aunt Kathleen gathering cackle berries. That rooster took umbrage to the fact that Jimmy had invaded his territory and flogged and spurred Jimmy, tearing his pants and scratching him on the face and arms. When Uncle Joe learned of the attack, he dispatched the rooster with his twelve-gauge shotgun. Dinner that Sunday was not exactly what the rooster had imagined it would be.

The third lesson was a messy one. On the farm there were two accepted methods of killing a chicken for the pot. The first was by wringing its neck. Using this method, one would grab the victim by its head and spin it, stopping the spin abruptly, and thus breaking the chicken's neck. The other method was less exacting but much more exciting. One would grab the chicken by both feet, place its head under foot, and quickly pull upward, disconnecting the head from the body, and then immediately toss the headless body, which would run around "like a chicken with its head off," spraying blood in all directions. This maneuver was very intriguing to a six-year-old boy, and after much pleading, Uncle Joe allowed me to try to dispatch a young fryer for Sunday dinner. Joe helped me grab the victim by the feet, placed its head under my foot, and said, "Pull." The first attempt failed. When I pulled, the chicken's head slipped from under my foot, and it pecked its way to freedom. After catching the escapee, Joe had a better idea. He would stand on the chicken's head and I would only have to pull, and pull, and pull! Finally, the chicken gave up its head. As it did so, I fell backward, flat on my back, forgetting to release the sacrifice. Joe and I both received a crimson shower. As I recall, that Sunday dinner was especially good, and even Aunt Kathleen commented on how nice it was to have a bird with an extra long neck.

June and the first two weeks of July of 1933 turned out to be hot and dry. Willie noted only two days of insignificant rain during that six-week period, and on Tuesday, June 6th, the thermometer climbed to a scorching ninety-seven degrees. The dry weather did allow the timely completion of corn planting. June 1st, Willie wrote: "Com Stafford was done planting corn."

Willie had worked for Commodore Chancey Stafford throughout the 1920s. Now Ray, Vernon, and Charles had taken over those jobs. The boys found work daily. Not only did they work for the Staffords, they were also employed as farmhands by the Sawlaws, Chet Hammond, the Kenny family, and Dwight Bright.

Most of the farming was done with horses. Tractors were new on the scene and very expensive. One of the first tractors used in Hunter Township was a Hauptman-Taylor, which was owned by Charles Ogle. The tractor was behemoth in size and was used to pull hedge rows. It was also utilized as a thrashing machine. The tractor could fly down the road at a blistering speed of two miles per hour. Heavy horses, Belgians and Percherons, were used for working the ground in the spring, planting, and then harvesting the crop. The Stafford family kept six to eight head of heavy horses year round. Paul Stafford, Com's son, recalls two light horses, mustangs, that his dad and uncle Ben had procured from out West. Paul said that they were two of the toughest horses he remembers. They could pull a corn planter all day long and needed very little rest. The heavier draft horses would work only a half-day. The teams that worked in the morning would be switched at noon for a fresh team. The lighter horses, although rarely used for heavy farm work, required less feed than their heavier counterparts. A mature draft horse weighs between 1,800 and 2,200 pounds, and that weight had to be maintained. Each day each horse would eat ten to twelve pounds of oats or oats mixed with cracked corn, a half bale of hay, and, depending on the weather conditions, drink at least thirty gallons of water. The horses were well cared for. They were brushed each day before they were harnessed. This allowed the handler to inspect for any sores the horse might have developed the previous day. Padding could then be utilized to prevent further damage that would render the horse useless. In the fall, teams of horses were used to pull the wagon that the handpicked corn was tossed into. One sideboard of this wagon was taller than the other, creating a bankboard. Thus, the men shucking the corn did not have to look as they tossed each ear over their shoulders into the wagon.

Consider this: Seventy years ago three men working three rows of corn with a wagon and a team of horses could hand shuck three hundred bushels of corn a day. As each wagon was loaded, the team of horses would be driven from the cornfield to a wire crib or frame granary. The wagon would then be unloaded by hand, using large scoop shovels to throw the ears of corn into the crib. In the thirties, the corn hiker was introduced. This labor-saving device was a metal conveyor that enabled the men unloading the corn to rake, rather than shovel, the ears of corn off the wagon. The workers would rake the corn into a triangle-shaped trough that was attached to the conveyor. From that trough, the conveyor would pick up the corn, "hiking" it into the crib or granary. Horsepower was also used to drive this mechanism. When the team of horses that was pulling the corn-laden wagon from the field reached the crib site, they would first be given a drink of water. The horses were then unhitched from the wagon and rehitched to a different horizontal tongue. That tongue was attached to a gear that drove a shaft, which turned a gear on the hiker. Thus, as the horses walked their slow, circuitous route, a chain reaction transferred the corn from the wagon to the crib. When the corn crop was finally in the crib, Mother Nature took over the drying process. It would be many years before artificial, on-the-farm drying methods would be introduced. After the corn dried, it still had to be husked and shelled before it could be sold to a grain dealer. This was yet another labor-intensive operation.

Now consider this. Today, for $150,000, give or take a few thousand dollars, one can purchase a combine with an eight-row corn-head that will pick, husk, and shell eighty to one hundred acres a day. That is three hundred bushels of corn in twenty minutes, and it is a one-man operation. In 1933, corn averaged forty bushel to the acre. An excellent crop yielded seventy bushel to the acre.

Today, in that same soil, corn will average 135 bushels per acre and, a really good crop will top 180 bushel to the acre. In 1933, corn was selling for sixty cents a bushel compared to today's price of $1.90.

By the mid-1930s, a new sound could be heard echoing across the prairies. The Farmall F12 and F14 tractors were introduced. Their cacophony would forever replace the neighing of the draft horses as farmers began to modernize and enlarge their farm operations. By the early 1950s, almost all of the gentle giants were retired to pasture if not sold off.

Many years ago, a misty-eyed Don Barkley told me the story of Mick and Molly. These were two Percherons that he had reared from foal. In 1946, a horse trader came through Edgar County, buying up retired draft horses. He approached Don and offered him a price for the team. Don, figuring the horses were not needed for the farm operations any longer, agreed on the price and sold Mick and Molly. The horses were loaded onto a truck and disappeared down the road. Later that night Don had second thoughts about the sale and reassessed his decision. The horses had been born on the farm, served him well for many years, and he now decided they should live out their remaining years in the pastures on the farm. Early the next morning he tracked the horses to the local stockyards only to find that the night before, the horses had been loaded onto railroad cars and moved west. Don eventually found his pair of horses and scores of others that had been doomed to the same fate in a rail yard at Mattoon, Illinois. He approached the buyer and offered to buy the team back at substantial profit for the horse trader. It was to no avail. The horses had been consigned to yet another party, and a very melancholy farmer returned home empty-handed.

It is obvious that reading this journal has stirred many memories. The entries into that journal may well have seemed mundane at the time, but seventy years later that is not the case. Those entries now stir memories of a time that many of us lived but present generations know little about. It is up to us grampas and grammas to explain to the youngsters how Willie's generation lived, to explain to them for example, what hauling coal by horse and wagon from the Interstate Coal Mine would have been like. That company was located just east of Baldwinsville on the Illinois-Indiana state line. Explain to them that Bud Hess delivered ice every Thursday and that the "spice man" visited regularly. How many of you remember the Watkins Man? Explain to the children why Willie's children would have walked six miles to town to swim at Tucker Beach. For entertainment at night he wrote of listening to WBOW from Terre Haute, Indiana, on a battery-powered AM radio. It seemed that those batteries powering the radio were constantly running out of juice. Every week or so, they would have to run to town to get the "Bee" battery recharged or, worse yet, buy a new one from Paul McFall for three bucks. Explain to the children that if the Downing family needed to use the phone, the only one available was up the road at Martin's Store. The company supplying that phone was the Wabash Telephone Company from St. Bernice, Indiana.

Some of us who are "growing a little long in the tooth" could write reams on the topics in the previous paragraph. I'll bet you a shiny copper that scores of children would enjoy listening to tales of bygone days.What may have seemed an unexciting venture seventy years ago turned out to be something wonderful, something valuable. William Wesley Downing left us a book, a book that reflects his love for and his pride in his family. It is a book that reveals exactly how life was for five months in 1933. Thanks, Willie!

"July 12 1933 wensday"

"The air is pretty cool to day and art went to coms to help thrash andvernon went to kennys to work and they finished thrashing wheat this afternoon and perry martin came down this afternoon a little while and harry brick ed dawson and miss pigg came up a while this afternoon and mrs crum and myrtle stoped a few minutes and thelma has got the mumphs jane and betty took the wash board home and mom washed to day for ourselves to day bud left some ice today"

That was the last journal entry. Willie died five days later.

" '...and', the king said very gravely, 'go on till you come to the end: then stop." Amen.

HUNTER'S MOON

The Indian nations used the moon and its phases as we use a calendar. Each time period or season began on a full moon, and each full moon had a name to coincide with the activity of that particular time of the year. Each year about this time, various tribes celebrated the hunter's moon.

For thirty or forty days before this moon, while their women and children finished gathering the various staples summer provided, the braves would prepare themselves for the approaching season by abstaining from eating any red meat. They also spent a significant amount of time in sweat lodges, forerunners of today's steam baths, purging their bodies of the evil spirits and the impurities produced by those who consume red meat. Four-legged creatures, especially those within the deer family, have exceptionally good noses, and the smell of a meat-eating predator would alert them immediately and set them fast afoot.

Like the Indians, our forefathers hunted out of necessity, and that instinct is surely passed down to this generation, although the need for hunting has disappeared. Is it any wonder why so many of us feel that primal urge to hunt, especially those of us who were reared in this rural area?

At this time of year, when the evenings are cooler, the smell of burning leaves is in the air, the apples have a livelier crunch that only a light frost can give them, the morning coffee tastes just a little better, and you hear before you ever see that first string of Canada geese winging so effortlessly southward to their wintering grounds, and you feel just a little better all over; it is autumn and autumn brings the hunting season.

It has been studied and reported on by perhaps Gene Hill or Richard Wolters or some other scribe that a hunter goes through several stages during his hunting career. The first stage begins when a youngster figures out where Dad is going before dawn and the "When can I go with you, Dad" question follows the elder out the door each and every trip. Finally, the day comes when the youngster is allowed to tag along but not quite ready to carry a gun but, perhaps, a sling-shot. I remember going squirrel hunting with Dad to Tuckers' Woods, at that time, Fay Moss Reeds woods. We would leave before first light and sit shivering in the woods under some likely nut tree until finally the sun would rise and sneak through the trees to at last warm us. We really did not shoot many squirrels as I recall. As a nine-year-old, I was more interested in "Why do some acorns have different kinds of hats on? Are we gonna dig sassafras later? How come some nuts are sweet and others so sour? Can we pick some paw-paws on the way home? Dad, how come we ain't seein' any squirrels?" We would eventually pack out of the woods, leaving the squirrels to ponder over my questions and go home to a hot breakfast and hot bath.

One morning as we were walking out of the woods, a rabbit burst from behind a log and streaked down the trail ahead of us. For some reason, Dad threw the old .22 single shot to his shoulder and let a round fly at the rabbit and nailed him square; a very lucky shot, not of course for the rabbit. Now this raised an immediate predicament: rabbits, it seems, were not in season. So here we were, pondering over what exactly to do with the rabbit. Dad was not about to leave him lie, and anyway, there could not be anyone within earshot. So, we picked up our supper and again sat out for the car. We hadn't gone fifty feet when we heard a voice from out of nowhere say, "Heck of a shot, Harry, but I have never seen a squirrel with ears that long". The voice was that of the Honorable George Bristow. For several seasons thereafter, we would run across Judge Bristow in those woods, and he would always bring up the long-eared squirrel.

The second stage in a hunter's career is the "How many can I bag?" stage. The new hunter has finally acquired a few tracking and calling skills, and bragging rights are the order of the day. Whether it be rabbits, quail, whatever, one is not satisfied unless he shoots a limit. This stage drives one to hunt long hours in all sorts of weather, in bitter cold, cold that even the prey itself would not venture out in. But we had to hunt and hunt we did; some of those bitter cold days we were successful, but more often than not, we were unsuccessful. The next stage is the "I'll only bag" stage. In this stage, one would only shoot at Mallard drakes or only hunt deer sporting twelve or more points on his rack. My ten-pointers are hanging now, reminding me of past hunts every time I enter the room in which they are hung. I have, it seems, entered the final stage.

Twenty years ago, I would never thought the day would come when I would say this, but I think the final stage a hunter goes through is his finest. Actually, it is not hunting, or at least doing very little of it. I shall always hunt, if for no other reason than to see my dogs work, but each year it seems we hunt less and less. I am more content to sit back and reminisce over past seasons and dogs long gone to their happy hunting grounds.

I still enjoy the friends that I have hunted with over the past forty years. I'll still go to the deer camp. I will still enjoy the breakfasts before each morning's duck hunt. And I really enjoy watching the youngsters that Uncle Don Farris and Brad Tucker have under their wing nowadays, some of the youngsters third-generation hunters who are dads I tutored thirty-five years ago. I started and taught their dads, just as Tom Sunken, Howard Anker, Uncle Benny Steidl and Allen Thomas carefully tutored me through my early hunting days. It is not that I do not care about hunting anymore. I savor every memory of hunting, but this year I will probably be just as content to pour four fingers of Old Bushmill and take it with my labs to the pasture and sit with the horse. Maybe we can catch the sound and sight of that first fall flight of Canadas winging it southward to Crab Orchard Lake. Have a good season.

THE DRIVE-INS

AFTER THE END OF WORLD War II, the American people began a love affair with the automobile. The mid-fifties saw the beginning of two-car family and with the coming of driving age of those entering their mid-teens. One of the most asked questions heard around the house was, "Dad, can I have the car tonight?"

The increase in the numbers of family cars and teenage drivers surely was a factor in the emergence of drive-in restaurants. In small towns across America, there was only so much a youngster could do on any given night if indeed he or she was offered the keys to the family car; and, more often than not, when one was given the keys, it was with the admonishment to not take the car out of town and "keep it off the gravel", The "keep it off the gravel" order served another purpose as well; it took the chance of parking on a country road out of play; thus, the young suitor had to use his imagination to find the more secret spots in the city to pursue his amorous ways. This, of course, was the beginning of what today is known as "cruising." Cruising in Paris was limited to driving between the parks and the various teenage hangouts, which include several drive-in restaurants. Let's journey back in time and visit those drive-ins that were so popular not only among teens but many adults as well.

Actually, the first drive-in I could find any record of was operated by Dale Sexton in 1937. The diner was located on Jasper Street and had an alley drive-through where one could pick up a bag of Mr. Sextons· specialty, barbecue beef sandwiches. Mr. Sexton was a far-sighted individual. It was many years later before the drive-in boom materialized to its vast popularity in the coming decades.

The new generation of drive-ins featured demure teenage lasses sporting the popular styles of the times, bobby sox and all. Now, Mom did not have to dress to the nines to grab a quick sandwich or a bag of burgers for the evening meal. She could order from the car, and typically of the era, a bobby-soxed teenage carhop would deliver her food straight to her car. The first drive-in Mom discovered in Paris was Phil's B and K. Phil Slifer, his wife, Norma, and brother Dale originated from Eau Claire County, Wisconsin. Phil was a route salesman for a local sausage company and later owned and operated two general stores. Norma owned two beauty shops. The Slifers were occasional patrons of a nearby A and W root beer stand near their hometown, and Phil had often expressed a desire to own a business that would give him the winters off. The couple investigated the root beer franchise business and eventually, after looking at locations in Indiana and Illinois, sold their businesses in Wisconsin and settled here in Paris.

On May 17, 1950, Phil and Norma opened the B and K root beer stand across from the water works on North Main Street. Phil and Dale built the building on ground leased from the Liggett family. Dale Slifer then went on to Georgetown, Illinois, and opened his own drive-in. The original drive-in was franchised from B and K. B and K are the initials of Mssrs. Burgesson and Kenifick. Mr. Burgesson was a schoolteacher and football coach in Wisconsin, and Mr. Kenifick was an attorney from Michigan City, Indiana. Their franchises extended throughout Michigan and Indiana, and Phil's B and K in Paris was their southernmost and first franchise in Illinois. The root beer syrup itself was manufactured by J. Hunterford Smith, a world-renowned, Tennessee-based company.

Norma's game plan was simple enough. She advised her staff to be especially kind to the youngsters and their elders who brought them to the drive-in. This nurtured a very faithful future clientele, because the very young she figured would mature into future customers as teens and later adults. The original drive-in had four carhops and two young men inside who would help wash glasses and set up trays. The first night the drive-in was open, they were so busy that Norma had to go outside to help wait on customers.

 Drive-in restaurants were totally new to the Paris area. People did not know what to expect, and Norma recalls that during that first busy evening, a car pulled in and she asked the man for his order. He replied, "We'll take two of anything you have to sell." He didn't even know what they had, but his order was filled. At that time, the menu consisted of hot dogs, barbecue hamburger, popcorn, soft ice cream and root beer.

The drive-in was closed from the last of September until the first of May each year. During the winter of 1954/1955, Phil tore down the original building. They moved back from the road and built a larger concrete-block building. That structure was the first in the B and K chain to sport an awning. The menu, it seems, grew as the business grew. Norma added ranch-burgers, french fries, cole slaw, and Barbecue Delights. In 1964, Norma enclosed the walk-in coolers and added the dining room to the north side of the building. With the new dining room came the addition of fish, tenderloins, chicken, steak, pizza burgers and chili. The drive-in by this time was a full-service restaurant supported by a staff of twenty-three, but the diner still retained the option of curb service. Memorial Day was the B and K's biggest day of the year. One Memorial Day alone they sold seven hundred and fifty gallons of root beer. In any given year, the drive-in would loose as many as fifteen cases of root beer mugs. Mug loss was a great concern of all the drive-in owners. The mugs were great collector items among teens; to get a mug from each of the several different stands was a coup, and the owners did all they could to discourage the liberating of those mugs.

On one occasion, Norma saw one youngster drive off with one of her baby mugs. She called the young man's parents before he got home; the next day brought the teen to apologize and return the errant mug. B and K was a true family business. The Slifers' three children worked there as well as Norma's brother and sister. Norma sold the B and K to Dave Pease in 1979. Fenton Cash later purchased the drive-in and has since torn it down to replace it by a more modern, convenient restaurant. Mrs. Slifer has since remarried and is enjoying retirement in Michigan.

Harold Mathis owned one of the first drive-ins in Paris. Harold purchased the Snack Bar from Holly Ogle in 1953. The drive-in was located at 624 N. Main and dates back to 1930, when Frank Thiele operated The Iron Lantern Coffee Shop. Mr. Mathis owned the drive-in until 1956. During those three years, Juanita Elledge Swinford and Sarah Dawson managed the business while Harold was employed full time at the Newport hard water plant at Newport, Indiana. Prior to the Snack Bar, Harold had owned the Illinois Cafe (1942) and was the first owner of the Snappy Service restaurant that adjoined the Lincoln Theater on North Central Avenue.

The Dog N Suds root beer was started in the mid-fifties in Champaign, Illinois, by two University of Illinois alumni. They opened the Paris operation in the summer of 1955. Coach John Stabler managed the drive-in. It was located across from the Edgar County Fairgrounds. Coach Stabler employed four carhops: Linda Eveland Shirar, Glenna Dee Johnson, Sally Melton and Beverly Warrick. Charlene, Coach's wife, cooked part time. Linda Shirar recalls that her hourly wage the summer of 1955 was twenty-five cents plus tips. The drive-in was very popular among teens, especially after Friday night football games. In 1956, Harold Mathis purchased the Dog N Suds and moved it to 114 Andrews, between the A&P grocery store and the Herm- Ermish dry cleaners. Harold sold the business a short time after that, and that operation was soon to shut down.

Later, in1965, a Mr. Barson from Erie, Pa., opened the franchise in a newer, state-of-the-art building that was designed and built by Paris's own Mr. Wm. Barnhart at the corner of Central and Jasper streets. The building featured indoor seating, and a large canopy covered the parking area. The newest innovation, however, was a speaker system, which allowed the customer to order over a two-way intercom from his car. This building design was used by the Dog N Suds Corp. nationwide. In 1969, Jim Keller took over the drive-in. Mr. Keller had three full-time and as many as ten part-time employees. Dianne Sims was the night manager. Bertha Perisho was responsible for the inside speaker phones, taking orders, then setting up the trays. Unlike the other drive-ins of the era, the Dog N Suds was open 365 days a year. Mr. Keller remembers that one of the most successful years the business had was 1970 and 1971. That was the season that Paris was contending for the basketball state championship, and Jim kept the school record posted on the marquee at the corner.

The Kellers sold out in 1973. Interestingly, a few years back, one of Jims' sales reps asked him if he would be interested in carrying the Dog N Suds root beer, which then and now comes in bottles and can be purchased from your local grocer. When the Dog N Suds closed in the seventies, it was the end of an era for the Paris area.

Just before 1956, Bert Trossen was getting fed up with the long hours of the automobile sales business and especially the harsh winters so common to the Marshfield, Wisconsin, area. The Trossens had visited with a friend from Texas who owned an A and W franchise, and he was pleased with the returns he was getting in addition to having winters off. So, Bert and his bride of twenty years, Geri, wrote to A and W seeking available franchises in the Illinois area. Mt. Carmel, Illinois, was the first town they investigated, but neither of them liked the location. On the way home, coming north on Illinois route one, they decided to stay over-night in Paris at the Pinnel Motel. The next morning, they were having coffee in the lobby of the motel; Geri looked across the highway and commented that it looked like a good location for their root beer stand. Bert thought it was too far out of town, but after some discussion, they agreed that Paris was the town and across from the motel was the spot for them. The necessary arrangements were made, and a nine-year success story began.

The A and W was a true drive-in restaurant by definition in that it had no indoor seating. When the patrons parked in one of the more than thirty spots available, they were greeted by a carhop dressed in black pants, white blouse, an A and W checkered vest and hat, and a pleasant "May I help you?" The carhops were local high school girls and boys, and during peak season as many as twenty-six were on the payroll at one time. The physical structure itself was suitably sized. The kitchen was in the rear of the building, and all of the appliances were situated in the exact position that expedited the finishing of fast food. In the front of the building was the set-up area for the trays as the orders were finished off. The front was totally surrounded in glass so that the parking areas could be monitored, but just as important, the customers could see in. Everything inside and out was kept spotless. In slack times, the carhops were kept busy keeping the parking areas free of debris. Those of us on the inside were always washing or spit-shining something.

Geri was the head cook, ably assisted by Nina Brosman and Peggy Cooper. The menu consisted of hot dogs, hamburgers, french fries, barbecue, onion rings, and hot tamales. A and W root beer and orange drink were pumped into ice-cold mugs, which came in three sizes: large, small and baby. One concoction that we served consisted of mixing one-half root beer and one-half orange drink, It was called a "Mike," being named after Mike Willison. Mike had worked the front end for several seasons and had started to draw himself a root beer but hit the orange instead. He went on to top the drink off with root beer, and a new drink was invented. During the peak hours, orderly bedlam reigned. The carhops were always in a frenzy, and the orders came to us inside as fast as they could tend each car. There was a unique choreography in the kitchen as well as up front. An inside worker had better know his area and what duties he was responsible for. If we accidentally stepped in front of someone and a tray was spilled … oh woe!! At times, orders would get lost. I remember one evening in the heat of battle, an order for a fish sandwich with tartar sauce was a little late coming out of the kitchen. I was standing by the window between the kitchen and the front, and Bert was directly behind me. Behind Bert was, as I recall, Donna Garver, who was busy pumping drinks. Bert hollered into the kitchen, "Where is my fish with tartar?" Geri immediately replied, "Here is your @#$#@ fish," as she threw it through the window at Bert. It barely missed me, missed Bert, the intended target, but caught Donna square in the back of the head. Two minutes later we were all laughing, the tension brought on by the rush having ebbed at once.

The two biggest evenings each season were the night of May Fete and the Fourth of July. On the Fourth, cars would line up on Route One to watch the fireworks, which were shot off from Twin Lakes Park. Those lines of cars would extend all the way north to Moss Road. One year alone on that holiday, we sold over three thousand ham sandwiches at ten cents each. On any given week, we would pump over six hundred gallons of root beer. The clientele varied by the hour of the day. At noon, it was mostly businesspeople and blue-collar workers. Then, at two-thirty every afternoon, an elderly gentleman we called Burger Basket would slowly drive up in his 1948 Dodge. His name we learned was Ben Crawford, and the girls would have his order waiting before he turned his motor off.

The evenings were when the fun began. From seven p.m. until closing time, scores of teens would circle the drive, cruising between Twin Lakes Park, downtown, the B and K and Clay Beach. The cars they drove were as unique as the individuals driving them. There were the family cars on loan for the night, the chopped and channeled coupes and a few street rods, the drivers of which, to Geri's dismay would pull the cut-out switch on their exhausts as they exited the drive-in, blasting the area with a raucous noise. There were very few cars with air conditioning at that time. The windows were always rolled down, and radios blared from stations like WLS from Chicago and WBOW from Terre Haute, Indiana, with the hits of the times: Elvis, The Big Bopper, Bill Haley and the Comets, Little Richard—well, you remember! Sometimes, when everyone cooperated, all of the car radios would be tuned to the same station, and the same songs could be heard no matter where you went in the parking lot.

A few of the choice parking spots were on the north side of the building facing the drive-in theater. One could park there, order a root beer and an order of onion rings and if Bert wasn't paying attention, which was seldom, sit for an hour or so and watch the movie playing next door at the drive-in theater. And Bert usually did pay attention. When he figured you had had enough time to eat and were just taking up space, he would have one of us ask the person to leave. Of course, all the driver would do is circle the lot a few laps then roost again.

The drive-ins were good places to look for girls and arrange later dates, and at least one romance I know of resulted in a marriage that has lasted until now. Kenny Garver frequented the A and W and became smitten by one of the carhops. Kenny first met Donna as she was hopping cars in 1958. I guess he liked the food. I know he liked Donna, because two years after meeting her at the A and W, on Donna's birthday, the tip he left her was an engagement ring. The A and W root beer stand was a success story. It was operated on family values. Hard work reaped just rewards. Bert always gave the kids who did not have transportation a ride home after work, many times in the wee hours of the morning.

Donna Garver states that the lesson that has stayed with her through the years is to not allow you to become overwhelmed, take one thing at a time. That lesson came from seeing lines of cars flood the parking lot after a major event downtown or at school. Bert and Geri sold out in 1965. The business had grown too big, and they wanted something smaller, less hectic. They moved to Jefferson, Iowa, a rural town with a population of 4,500. Ironically, the A and W they started there grew larger than the Paris operation. The Trossens eventually retired to Florida. Bert has since passed on. Geri is in good health, enjoying retirement.

In the late fifties and early sixties, there were several other drive-ins in Paris, George Papadokas ran the Coney Island across from the entrance to Twin Lakes Park. The Dairy Delight was just north of the water works, in front of Bill Sutton's roller rink. Roy and Fern Coogan had a soft-serve ice cream stand where McDonalds is situated today. Jim and Marie Pope ran the Dairy Queen near the fairgrounds. And although those mentioned above were not of the same type, in that they did not have carhops and were not popular teen hangouts, they should be mentioned. Most of them specialized in soft-serve ice cream. One of the pioneers of the soft-serve business was Perry Piper. The following information was obtained from an article Perry wrote in 1993, for the Marshall Choice.

Mr. Piper opened Dairy Land, on the corner of Jasper and Jefferson streets, the summer of 1950. Blanche Henson was the manager. Blanche had previously worked for the Equity Dairy Bar, and with her experience and the new product, Dairy land became an instant success. A year later, Farm Bureau decided they needed the location, and Mr. Piper was forced to relocate at 1600 S. Main. On S. Main, the Pipers built a much larger building that featured both window service as well as inside seating for thirty-six patrons at a double horseshoe bar and booths. At first they served only shakes and ice cream, but as the business grew, they became a full short-order facility that was open 365 days a year. Mrs. Piper was enlisted to make barbecue. They mixed their own root beer in fifty-gallon lots, and each season sold hundreds of gallons of it dispensed into frosty mugs. One of the most popular items offered was the Sampler. It consisted of five sundaes in one dish, each with a different topping. The sundae sold for 49 cents and the customer got to keep the dish. Tilton Piper remembers on one occasion, the drive-in featured banana splits. They purchased two stalks of bananas and hung them in front of the building. When the customer arrived, he could pick his own banana and take it to the window where the dish would be completed. Tilton said that by the time they closed that evening, there were banana peels all over the south side of town. The seventies saw the end of most of the drive-in restaurants as we knew them in the fifties. Times were changing, and drive-ins were not so much drive-in as they were drive-through. Teens still congregate of an evening but in different locales. Terre Haute and Charleston are closer because of better roads, and with driver's education mandatory at every high school, today's teen is likely to be a more knowledgeable driver than those of the early fifties. Thus, parents are more likely to grant permission for out-of-town trips. That permission was hard to get in the fifties.

One drive-in in this area has survived for the past thirty-six years. The Frost Top in Chrisman, owned by the Riggen family, still uses carhops and serves homemade sandwiches and root beer. Want to relive part of your past? Some evening, hop in your jalopy, leave the windows down—no air conditioning allowed. Find a fifties radio station, and turn the volume up two or three notches more than your old ears can stand. Cruise through the countryside to Chrisman and enjoy the Frost Top. Maybe you can even talk Rena into making you a Mike.

BIOGRAPHY

HARRY PARRISH WAS BORN AND reared in Edgar County, Illinois. He resides there on the edge of the Grand Prairie just north of Paris, Illinois with his wife of thirty-seven years, Beverly Michael Parrish.

Mr. Parrish started writing as a hobby in 1993. His primary interests at that time were the events leading to the founding of Paris, Illinois which was the county seat of Edgar County. Those articles relate stories dating from 1780 to the present. Each story took months of research and reflect Harry's love of each project and his tenacity to accurately detail each event.

In the fall of 2008, Harry wrote his first children's book entitled KATE AND ALICE. He is currently working on a children's adventure book which will be published by Authorhouse in the summer or early fall of 2009.

Mr. Parrish trains and races harness horses during the spring and summer months. He races at Balmoral Park in Crete, Illinois, Indiana Downs at Shelbyville, Indiana, and at Bluegrass Downs in Paducah, Kentucky as well as many of the county fairs in Illinois. Mr. Parrish trains trotters at the Edgar County fair grounds which is located in Paris, Illinois. He writes during his off-season each year.